P9-ECJ-798

YUMA COUNTY
LIBRARY DISTRICT
2951 S. 21st Dr. Yuma, AZ 85364
(928) 782-1871
www.yumalibrary.org

DISCARDED
BY
Yuma County Library District

Chloe
FLAVOR

SAUCY
CRISPY
SPICY
VEGAN

Chloe FLAVOR

Chloe Coscarelli

CLARKSON POTTER/PUBLISHERS
New York

for the animals

CONTENTS

FOREWORD by Michael Symon

I know what you're probably thinking: *What's a guy like me doing introducing a vegan cookbook?*

I'm a passionate longtime chef, restauranteur, author, TV personality . . . and a die-hard carnivore through and through. (Seriously, I even wrote a book about it!) So naturally you'd think I'd be the first guy in line to be making fun of vegans, not endorsing their recipes, right? Well, here are a couple facts you may not know about me. My lovely bride of twenty years is a vegetarian and I actually *love* vegetables. Add to this that I know a chef like Chloe and the fact that she has changed how I feel about vegan cooking forever.

Chloe appeared on my food talk show, *The Chew*, back in 2016, and the other hosts and I had the opportunity to try some of her vegan offerings. I have to admit I was skeptical when I met this cheerful young woman sporting a pink chef's jacket and parading out tray after tray of food. Bacon made out of mushrooms? Bean burgers? Cheese made from sweet potatoes? It all looked good, but what would it taste like? I had no idea what to expect.

Then I took my first bite.

The shiitake mushroom bacon was smoky and crispy, the black bean and quinoa burger was hearty and charred to perfection, and the sweet potato cheese sauce on Chloe's mac and cheese was velvety smooth and full of melty, savory goodness. I'm telling you, this was some amazing stuff! Chloe Coscarelli helped open my mind to the possibilities of vegan cooking. What Chloe was doing with food was some of the craziest, most innovative stuff I had ever seen come out of any kitchen, vegan or not.

She really did prove that you can have all the rich, complex, comforting flavors of familiar foods, without the traditional animal ingredients. Who would have thought plants—remixed into new versions of America's favorite dishes—would blow my mind?

Despite our differences in cooking, Chloe and I have something major in common: a devotion to flavor and the pursuit of creating easy, delicious recipes everyone can make and enjoy. If you're wary of vegan food and think it can't be flavorful or interesting, trust me and think again.

Chloe's recipes are a way for my wife, Liz, and I to continue to connect over something we both love: great food! We can feast together on things like Apricot-Sesame Cauliflower Wings, Tangy Maple BBQ Burgers, and, yes, even a Bacon Lover's vegan BLT without sacrificing killer flavor. Chloe and other vegan chefs are at the forefront of a culinary revolution that is helping us realize that healthy food and delicious food can, and should, go hand in hand.

If you've picked up this book as a longtime vegan or vegetarian, you'll be thrilled with the many inventive, tasty recipes that Chloe has cooked up for you. But if you're reading this book as someone who's just thinking about getting a few more vegetables into your diet, consider this: *Chloe Flavor* is a great place to start. Look, I'm always going to enjoy eating and cooking meat, but if a carnivore like me can be sold on the idea of a bean burger, maybe you can be, too.

Live to Cook,

MICHAEL

INTRODUCTION

Hello again—Chloe here. I'm beyond excited you've opened up *Chloe Flavor,* my fourth cookbook! To those of you who've already cooked with me in my previous books, it's great to see you again. I hope you find this book to be the best one yet! To my new friends, nice to meet you and welcome aboard my culinary journey. I hope *Chloe Flavor* awakens your very best inner chef and wows your taste buds with flavors like never before.

my journey to vegan

Let's back up a little. Why vegan? I'm a born-and-bred animal lover. My family has adopted every abandoned animal that has crossed our path. Growing up, I always watched my parents hit the car brakes for stray dogs and cats, fallen birds, or any living, breathing being that looked injured or in need of help. We found our sweet family dog Harriet in a Payless Shoes parking lot with a dirty rope around her neck, and our beloved Chi babies, Winnie and Buster, came out of a cardboard box at a gas station (we said we would just foster them, and well, you know how that turns out). We always had at least four adopted pets at a time—even rats. (I swear, they are the cutest, sweetest, most loving little beings on earth!)

But even while we loved and cherished the animals in our home, we still ate meat. It never struck me as odd—until it did. And one day it hit me. I realized there was no difference between my pets and the animals on my dinner plate and I decided then and there to go vegan. This means that I don't eat anything that comes from an animal (no meat, no fish, no dairy, and no eggs), but the real beauty of veganism lies in all the things I *can* eat. Hello, Mango Guacamole Crunch Burgers (page 122) and Black Forest Cherry Cake (page 222)!

When I went vegan, I was sixteen years old. That was in what I call the "pre-kale" days, when no one looked further than mashed potatoes or steamed broccoli for a vegetable side and vegan mac and cheese was a concept that had not yet arrived on this planet. If a vegan wanted to eat, well, then she had to cook!

Lucky for me, my mom taught me how. She's an incredible cook and we've always been inseparably close. I grew up sitting on the kitchen counter, watching her do her thing, sometimes helping, always tasting. When I went vegan, she supported me 100 percent of the way. She cooked me a separate Thanksgiving meal and she even found a vegan cooking class for us to go to two hours from our house. Every one of the zillions of meals we've cooked and eaten together bonds us at the core. To this day, there isn't a recipe I've created I haven't discussed with her at length.

never giving up

Since writing my last book, a lot has happened in my life and in my kitchen. The past few years have been a roller coaster, and with every passing day I've grown more and more committed to my craft and my cause. While girls my age were saving for their dream weddings, I put every penny I had into commercial kitchen shelving and stainless-steel prep tables in my apartment. I didn't want new clothes or shoes; I wanted a professional-grade ice cream maker and a Vitamix XL.

I have been lucky enough to experience honors and successes in my career. I cooked the first-ever sold-out all-vegan dinner at South Beach Wine and Food Festival with trailblazing plant-based chef Matthew Kenney. It was one of the most magical nights of my life to see our vegan menu (complete with beet ravioli and cashew alfredo) garner praise, especially since the festival is generally a pretty meaty affair. I also had the honor of checking off an item on every chef's bucket list: cooking at the James Beard House. (On top of that, it was the very first ethical vegan dinner the foundation had ever hosted!) I cooked with three other rock star vegan chefs and the event sold out in less than twenty-four hours. It's safe to say we brought the house down and nobody missed the meat!

And as life goes, with the highs came some devastating setbacks. I poured my blood, sweat, and onion tears into opening my very first restaurant in New York City. While I was proud of the menu I created and from the outside it appeared to be a success, it turned out to be an incredibly difficult and disappointing experience. I learned a lot about myself and my own strength and, most important, that I'm truly dedicated to sharing delicious vegan food with the world and proving that animals don't need to suffer in order for humans to eat tasty, flavorful meals. I will forever be grateful to everyone who has and continues to support me in that journey. My favorite quote right now is from late German political activist Sophie Scholl: "Stand up for what you believe in, even if you are standing alone." Amen, sister.

my philosophy on food

Since I first went vegan, veganism has come a long way, and I'm proud to have been part of that evolution. Today, corner stores stock their shelves with kale chips and mainstream restaurants pepper their menus with quinoa, tempeh, chia seeds, farro, ramps, and so many variations of avocado toast. There is truly no better time to love to eat than now—and no easier time to be a vegan.

When I first decided to be a vegan chef, I had a dream of changing the way the world eats. Sweet little piglets crisped up into bacon strips on a brunch plate? But *why?!* Just in the name of flavor? What if we could make even better flavors out of sweet, crispy, creamy, saucy, beautiful, plant-based ingredients? Every recipe in this book is an expression of my love for Earth's phenomenal ability to grow the coolest, most perfect ingredients in all shapes and colors from the ground up.

So where do we begin? It is my mission to show you how to bring all the delicious culinary inspiration and innovation from cuisines around the world right into your own kitchen. Whether you've never boiled water or you consider your *brunoise* skills Michelin-star worthy, whether you're a chard-loving vegan or die-hard burger lover, if you love flavorful, hearty, mind-blowing meals, this book has something for you.

I have personally tested and tweaked each recipe tens to hundreds of times (really!), because I'd rather make all the mistakes so you can succeed. Nobody is making a bad meal on my watch, and that is a promise. I'm reachable at all hours on social media if you have any questions while you cook, so don't hesitate to ask! I've got your back.

my advice to you

The single most important thing that gets me through even the craziest challenges in life is ending each day with good food and good people. Being an entrepreneur is chaotic, so I've been spending more and more time cooking for family and friends at home, often insisting on a sweatshirts-and-yoga-pants dress code to keep it low key. We gather around my tiny kitchen table, drink inexpensive wine, and indulge in nourishing Red Thai Curry (page 187) or Spicy Rigatoni Vodka (page 151). A home-cooked meal sparks the most intimate conversations and connects you to your guests in an endorphin-releasing kind of way. All of the recipes in this book are preapproved by my friends and family and are ready for yours. So what are you waiting for?

Life's too short. Express yourself in the kitchen. Nothing says "I love you" more than cooking a meal for someone special. Don't be afraid to fail. If you don't push the boundaries of your cooking, you're holding out on your very best creations. As you cook through this book, go off-road from the recipes and make them your own. The beauty of vegan cooking is in what's yet to be created. Holy shiitake, let's do this!

XO *Chloe*

THE VEGAN KITCHEN

What makes a great vegan kitchen? The chef, of course! But aside from that, here are a few tips to set yourself up for culinary success.

ingredients

NUTS

Nuts of all kinds, whether almonds, cashews, walnuts, pine nuts, or pistachios, are essential to vegan cooking, and make wonderful substitutes for cream and cheese. When blended with water and other flavors, cashews can turn into a creamy Alfredo sauce (page 149) or luscious mac-and-cheese sauce (page 148). I recommend always having raw cashews on hand, as they are my favorite and will come up in many of these recipes.

fats and oils

OLIVE OIL

Olive oil is rich in antioxidants and vitamin E. It is a great source of heart-healthy monounsaturated fat and helps to lower cholesterol. Olive oil is a good choice for medium-heat cooking, such as sautéing and browning. It is also great in salad dressings and sauces, and for drizzling on finished dishes. I prefer extra-virgin olive oil, which comes from the first pressing of olives, making it the purest in taste and least acidic.

VEGETABLE OIL

In recipes that call for vegetable oil, any neutral-tasting, mild oil that is suitable for baking or high-heat cooking will do. This includes canola oil, refined coconut oil, safflower oil, and grapeseed oil, all of which are excellent choices for cooking, baking, or frying at high temperatures.

TIP THAT'S NUTTY

Blending nuts with water is a technique I use often to make luscious, dairy-free creams that serve as a base for sauces, soups, or desserts. If you have a high-powered blender (see page 17), you can blend your nuts raw without any kind of soaking. If you do not have a high-powered blender, you can try using them raw, but if you have trouble, soak the nuts overnight or in boiling water for 10 minutes, then drain them before blending. This will soften them and ensure a silky-smooth cream once blended.

COCONUT OIL

Coconut oil, which is pressed from copra (dried coconut meat), is one of the few saturated fats that does not come from an animal and is actually very healthful. It is high in lauric acid, which has many antiviral, antibacterial, and antioxidant properties that fight illnesses such as heart disease, diabetes, cancer, and HIV. It is also cholesterol- and trans-fat-free. Because coconut oil is quite heat stable, it is perfect to use for high-heat cooking or frying. It can keep on your pantry shelf for up to two years.

Coconut oil is solid at room temperature, which makes it great for baking because many pastry recipes call for solidified fat (i.e., butter!). Unrefined coconut oil (same as "virgin") has a coconut flavor, while refined coconut oil does not. Feel free to substitute coconut oil for vegan margarine or vegetable shortening in equal quantities in any recipe. It works especially well as a substitute in my frostings and cookies.

VEGAN MARGARINE

Vegan margarine is a terrific stand-in for butter in vegan cooking and baking. My favorite brands are Earth Balance and Miyoko's Kitchen, which can be purchased in sticks or in a tub. They are natural, nonhydrogenated, and trans-fat-free. You can buy vegan margarine at your local grocery store.

VEGETABLE SHORTENING

Shortening is a solidified blend of oils that is great for making creamy frostings and flaky piecrusts. To be sure you are choosing the most healthful option, look for packaging labeled "nonhydrogenated." Spectrum Organics and Earth Balance are excellent brands.

flavorings

HERBS

Herbs are essential to flavorful vegan cooking, and I use both fresh and dried. It's a good idea to keep a pantry stocked with some basic dried herbs. If you ever need to substitute, use one part dried to three parts fresh. I keep the following dried herbs in my pantry at all times: basil, thyme, rosemary, and oregano.

NUTRITIONAL YEAST FLAKES

Not to be confused with brewer's yeast, active dry yeast, or instant yeast, nutritional yeast has a roasted, nutty, cheeselike flavor. It is a good source of amino acids and B vitamins, and most brands are naturally gluten-free. Nutritional yeast is what gives my Cashew Queso (page 119) its yellow color and cheesy flavor. You can find nutritional yeast in the bulk aisle in most natural foods markets, or in the supplements/wellness section. Bob's Red Mill and Bragg are excellent brands that can also be purchased online.

SALT

Salt brings out and brightens the flavors of food. I like to cook with fine-grain sea salt, which is unrefined, unbleached, and rich in health-supportive trace minerals. The taste is also far superior to white table salt. Coarse or flaky sea salt is a nice finishing salt.

TAMARI

Tamari is a wheat-free variety of soy sauce that adds flavor, saltiness, and color to many vegan dishes. Purchase gluten-free tamari when cooking gluten-free. San-J is a popular brand.

VINEGAR

Vinegar adds tanginess and flavor to any food. When combined with baking soda, it is used frequently in vegan baking to replace eggs, as it helps baked goods bind together and rise. The types of vinegar I recommend keeping on hand are apple cider (for baking), balsamic (for finishing), and seasoned rice (for Asian dishes).

BEETS

Roasted beets are an incredible root vegetable that I use for many different purposes. They lend a gorgeous bright pink color to anything they are mixed with, making them a perfect choice in sauces, grain and pasta dishes, or really anything that can pick up color. You can save yourself some time by buying packaged pre-roasted beets—I like Love brand—or roasting up a big batch and keeping them on hand.

TIP CATCH THAT BEET

To roast beets, preheat the oven to 400°F. Wash and scrub the beets and pierce them all over with a fork. Drizzle with olive oil and wrap loosely in aluminum foil. Bake for about 1½ hours, or until fork-tender. Let cool completely, then trim, peel, and measure out the amount of roasted beet needed for your recipe.

flours

WHEAT FLOURS

There are a variety of flours to use in cooking and baking. Many of my recipes call for unbleached all-purpose flour. This is regular white flour, and it yields a light and tender product. I use it in cakes, muffins, and cookies. Whole-wheat pastry flour is an unrefined alternative to all-purpose flour. For any quantity of all-purpose flour, you can use a mix of half whole-wheat pastry flour and half all-purpose flour if you prefer.

GLUTEN-FREE FLOUR

Gluten-free flour is just what it sounds like. Fear not, gluten-free bakers, the gluten-free flour selection at the grocery store is expanding by the minute. Bob's Red Mill Gluten-Free 1-to-1 Baking Flour is my favorite product that can be substituted measure-for-measure in many of my recipes. It is made from a blend of rice flour and potato starch, and can be found at your local grocery store or ordered online at bobsredmill.com. I also love gluten-free oat flour and almond flour, which lend a subtle earthy flavor. When substituting gluten-free flour in a recipe, make sure the other ingredients you are using in the recipe are gluten-free as well.

grains

The most common grains are wheat, rice, rye, barley, and corn. Quinoa is considered a super grain; it is a complete protein because it contains all eight essential amino acids.

legumes

The legume family includes beans, lentils, peas, and peanuts. They are a good source of protein and fiber in any diet, including a vegan diet.

meat and dairy substitutes

TOFU

Commonly used in vegetarian cooking, tofu is high in protein and iron and very low in calories and fat. It is made from soybeans and will take on the flavor of any dressing, marinade, or sauce, making it a versatile meat substitute. There are two kinds of tofu that I like to cook with: soft (or silken) and extra-firm. Soft tofu is great for blending into salad dressings or dips. Extra-firm tofu can be crumbled, baked, and stir-fried. Any leftover tofu can be kept in an airtight container in the refrigerator, covered with fresh water, for up to five days; change the water every two days. Tofu also freezes well. When thawed, the texture is firm and chewy, which makes it perfect for savory dishes. My favorite brand is Nasoya.

TIP IM-PRESS-IVE TOFU

To press your tofu, wrap it tightly in kitchen or paper towels and place a heavy object (i.e., a can of coconut milk or a few cookbooks) on top. Let sit for about 20 minutes while excess water is released from the tofu. Unwrap and cut into the size called for in the recipe. Now your tofu is ready to soak up all the juices and flavors of your dish!

TEMPEH

Tempeh (pronounced *TEM-pay*) is a fermented soy product that is extremely high in protein and fiber. It originates from Indonesia and has a nutty texture and mild flavor. Don't be alarmed if you see black spots on your tempeh; that is a completely normal sign of the fermentation process. Opened packages of tempeh will keep for up to ten days in the refrigerator and up to three months in the freezer. Tempeh can be crumbled, sliced, diced, or marinated. Find it in the refrigerated section of your local natural foods market, next to the tofu.

SEITAN

Seitan (pronounced *SAY-tan*) is made from the protein in wheat flour called gluten. It is chewy and hearty, and soaks up savory sauces very well. It is made from a simple process of mixing wheat flour and water, and you can buy it packaged in the refrigerated section at your local natural foods market. If you want to make your own seitan from scratch, check out the recipe in my first book, *Chloe's Kitchen*.

MUSHROOMS

Mushrooms are the only vegetable that I am addressing as a "meat substitute" because they have a juicy and meaty texture, making them a fabulous choice in vegan cooking. They are rich in antioxidants, protein, and fiber. Mushrooms are also a great source of minerals, such as selenium, that fight heart disease and cancer. Choose mushrooms that are firm and dry, and wipe them clean with a damp towel. (Don't soak them—they'll absorb water and become soggy.) Trim the stem ends of all mushrooms before using, remembering that the stems of shiitake mushrooms are not edible. The mushrooms I use most frequently are cremini, portobello, shiitake, oyster, and porcini.

ALMOND MILK

Almond milk is made from pulverized almonds and water. The almond flavor is very subtle. Almond milk is thick and has added vitamins, such as calcium and vitamin D. It has no saturated fat, is cholesterol-free, and very low in calories. Many of my recipes call for almond milk, simply because that is my personal favorite, but feel free to substitute other varieties of nondairy milk such as rice, soy, hemp, oat, and coconut milk.

COCONUT MILK

Coconut milk is thick and creamy, making it a great nondairy milk to use in Asian sauces, curries, and desserts. The fat in coconut milk is a healthful, good fat, does not contribute to heart disease, and is beneficial to the cardiovascular system. You can buy coconut milk canned or in cartons in the refrigerated section of your grocery store. I prefer to use full-fat canned coconut milk, which is slightly thicker. My favorite brands are Thai Kitchen and Whole Foods 365 brand.

TIP SHAKE IT UP!

Separation of the coconut cream and the coconut water often occurs in cans of coconut milk. When a recipe calls for a measured amount of canned coconut milk, make sure that you shake or stir it very well *before* measuring, so that your measured amount consists of smooth coconut milk, as opposed to being too watery or heavy on the cream.

pasta

Dried pasta is almost always vegan, except for egg noodles. Fresh pasta, on the other hand, is commonly made with egg. You can use regular wheat pasta ("white" pasta), or you can sub whole-wheat or gluten-free alternatives. There are many gluten-free dried pasta options including brown rice pasta, quinoa pasta, chickpea pasta, lentil pasta, and black bean pasta. Sub freely.

sweeteners

SUGAR

When choosing granulated or confectioners' sugar for baking, I look for words like *organic*, *fair trade*, and *vegan* on the package because some refined sugars are processed using animal bone char. Wholesome Sweeteners, Florida Crystals, and Whole Foods store brand are all good-quality brands of unrefined vegan sugars.

AGAVE NECTAR

Agave nectar is a natural, unrefined liquid sweetener that is extracted from the leaves of the Mexican agave plant. Agave has a sweeter flavor than sugar and a lower glycemic index, too, which means it won't spike your blood sugar. I prefer to use light agave because of its milder flavor and clear color, but you can also buy it in darker varieties.

MAPLE SYRUP

Pure maple syrup is a natural, unrefined sweetener that is good for more than just pouring over pancakes. Its distinct taste can enhance many savory dishes, for example, Sausage Links (page 44), and baked goods, such as Banana Doughnuts with Maple Glaze (page 238). Grade B is great for baking and darker in color than Grade A.

thickeners

XANTHAN GUM

Xanthan gum is a fine powder used for thickening, stabilizing, and emulsifying. I use xanthan gum when making ice cream from scratch because it adds a thick and stretchy quality to the ice cream.

CORNSTARCH

A fine powder made from corn kernels, cornstarch is used as a thickener in sauces, gravies, and custards. Buy organic to ensure your cornstarch is non-GMO.

baking

CHOCOLATE CHIPS

I use semisweet chocolate chips in many of my dessert recipes. Many brands, such as Enjoy Life or Guittard, make dairy-free semisweet chocolate chips. Look for bags labeled *dairy-free* or *vegan*.

UNSWEETENED COCOA POWDER

There are two types of cocoa powder: Dutch-process and natural. Dutch-process cocoa powder goes through a procedure to alkalize the cocoa, giving it a richer and less bitter flavor. I prefer Dutch-process and recommend Valrhona and Droste brands. Most important, make sure your cocoa powder is unsweetened—no sugary hot cocoa mix, please!

INSTANT ESPRESSO POWDER

Espresso powder is a very dark and strong instant coffee. I use it in many of my dessert recipes for flavoring—for example, it enhances the taste of chocolate. I use Medaglia d'Oro brand, which can be found in the coffee aisle at any grocery store or purchased online. If you cannot find espresso powder, substitute the same amount of finely ground instant coffee. You may also use decaffeinated if you prefer.

FLAVORED EXTRACTS

Adding a teaspoon or two of flavored extract is a great way to intensify flavor. When purchasing extracts, look for the word *pure* (such as "pure vanilla extract" or "pure almond extract") on the label to avoid artificial flavors and chemicals. I always keep vanilla, almond, and peppermint extracts on hand.

COCONUT

Shredded coconut, chopped coconut, or coconut flakes add extra flavor and texture to coconut cakes and pies. Feel free to use sweetened or unsweetened. Toasting it adds a little extra crunch to your dessert. Spread coconut on a rimmed baking sheet and bake at 350°F for 5 to 10 minutes, or until golden, turning frequently with a spatula to ensure even browning.

MARSHMALLOWS

Marshmallows aren't always vegan; many of the mainstream brands use gelatin, which is derived from animals. Instead, buy vegan marshmallows, which are gelatin-free. Sweet & Sara and Dandies are my two favorite brands, and can be found in natural foods markets or online.

SPRINKLES

Sprinkles are one of my all-time favorite ingredients to beautify any dessert. But did you know that not all sprinkles are vegan? Many are made with beeswax, gelatin, and even crushed insects for coloring. I know, it's heartbreaking. But have no fear, my favorite all-vegan sprinkle brand, Sweetapolita, is here! Just visit sweetapolita.com for rainbow, chocolate, and even holiday-themed sprinkley goodness in all shapes and sizes.

equipment

BLENDER

A blender is an important tool for making sauces, soups, and ice creams. You can use any type of blender for the recipes in this book. My favorite is a Vitamix, a very high-speed, heavy-duty machine, available in kitchen supply stores and online. A less powerful blender will work just fine; just be sure to stop periodically and scrape down the sides with a spatula while blending. A food processor will usually work in place of a blender, except when blending nuts into a cream (see Tip, page 11).

FOOD PROCESSOR

A food processor is a workhorse in any kitchen. It can help you take many shortcuts by making pasta dough, chopping nuts, grating zucchini, grinding chocolate, and so on. I recommend getting at least an 11-cup capacity food processor, although you can always work in batches with a smaller one.

PARCHMENT PAPER

Available in both rolls and sheets, parchment paper is coated with silicone to make it nonstick. Use it on baking sheets to prevent your treats from sticking. I prefer parchment paper to wax paper, because wax paper is not always oven-safe.

STAND OR HANDHELD MIXER

Electric stand mixers are useful for kneading dough, mixing batters, and beating frostings. If you don't have the space for a stand mixer, a handheld electric mixer and a large bowl will work, too.

ICE CREAM MAKER

Ice cream makers come in a range of shapes, sizes, and prices. You do not need to buy an expensive industrial version to make my recipes.

ICE CREAM & COOKIE SCOOPS

Ice cream and cookie scoops are great for scooping dough and batter evenly onto baking sheets or into cupcake pans. This will give your baked goods a professional, uniform look.

TIP THE MOST IMPORTANT INGREDIENT IS CREATIVITY!

Ready, set, let's cook! There are times when even *I* realize I don't have a certain ingredient or piece of equipment I need to complete a recipe. Use your best judgment to see if you can get creative with a solution. Whether it's substituting thyme for rosemary or using a spoon instead of a specific size ice cream scoop, more often than not, you can make a recipe work.

Ladies and gentlemen, start your ovens!

but first

BREAKFAST
& BRUNCH

AVOCADO PESTO TOAST

SERVES 2

1 **avocado**

2 cups **fresh basil**

2 tablespoons **olive** or refined **coconut oil**, plus more for drizzling

1 tablespoon **lemon juice**

½ teaspoon **sea salt**

Freshly ground **black pepper**

4 slices **whole-grain bread**

Crushed red pepper flakes

I included a recipe for avocado toast in my very first cookbook in 2012, inspired by one of my favorite cafés in New York City, Café Gitane. According to my mom, I "invented" it! The truth is avocado toast is not an invention, but instead an ever-evolving medium for avocado-lovers to get their fix. In this version, I get in touch with my Italian roots and incorporate garlic, basil, and lemon. I love this for breakfast, or also as an appetizer with lunch or dinner. Three tips: (1) Use a hearty seeded bread. (2) Be very generous with your crushed red pepper sprinkling. (3) Serve this hot off the griddle—no soggy toast, please!

MAKE IT GLUTEN-FREE: Use gluten-free bread.

In a food processor, combine the avocado, basil, olive oil, lemon juice, and salt. Season generously with black pepper and blend until smooth.

Heat a small skillet or griddle over medium-high heat. Drizzle the bread with olive oil on both sides, and when the skillet is hot, place the bread in it and toast until crispy and golden, about 2 to 3 minutes per side.

Transfer the toast to a plate, spread a thin layer of avocado pesto on one side, and top with crushed red pepper. Serve immediately.

BREAKFAST COOKIES

MAKES 15 COOKIES

1 cup all-purpose **flour** or **whole-wheat pastry flour**

½ teaspoon **baking soda**

¼ teaspoon **sea salt**

½ cup **coconut oil** or **vegan margarine**

½ cup packed **light brown sugar**

2 tablespoons **creamy almond butter**

1 tablespoon **water**, plus more if needed

2 teaspoons **pure vanilla extract**

½ cup **rolled oats**

¼ cup unsweetened **shredded coconut**

¼ cup **dried cranberries**

¼ cup chopped pitted **Medjool dates** (about 5 dates)

1 tablespoon **chia seeds**

Confectioners' sugar, for dusting

If sugary cereals and doughnuts can count as breakfast foods, surely these healthful cookies do, too. Made with protein-packed almond butter, oats, chia seeds, and dates, these cookies would be a great start to your morning, or a lunchbox item or snack.

MAKE-AHEAD TIP: The cookie dough can be made in advance, pre-scooped, and stored in an airtight container in the refrigerator for up to 5 days or in the freezer for up to 1 month. If baking from frozen, let them bake an extra few minutes.

MAKE IT GLUTEN-FREE: Use gluten-free baking flour, gluten-free oats, and gluten-free coconut.

Preheat the oven to 350°F. Line a large baking sheet with parchment paper.

In a small bowl, whisk together the flour, baking soda, and salt. Set aside.

In a stand mixer fitted with the whisk attachment or in a large bowl using a handheld mixer, beat together the coconut oil, brown sugar, almond butter, water, and vanilla until fluffy. Slowly beat in the flour mixture. Fold in the oats, shredded coconut, cranberries, dates, and chia. If the dough seems dry, add more water, a teaspoon at a time, and beat again.

Scoop about 2 tablespoons of dough at a time onto the prepared baking sheets, placing them about 3 inches apart.

Bake for about 12 minutes, until the edges are golden. Let cool on the baking sheet and lightly dust with confectioners' sugar.

ALMOND BUTTER BERRY BOWL

SERVES 2

2 frozen **bananas**

½ cup frozen **blueberries**

1 tablespoon **almond butter**

Almond milk

optional toppings

Maple-Pecan Granola (recipe follows) or store-bought granola

Fresh berries

Unsweetened **shredded coconut**

Chia seeds

Vegan chocolate chips

When I make this dish for kids, I call it "Breakfast Ice Cream." It's vibrant, delicious, and, well, tastes just like ice cream! You can top it with any kind of fruit, nuts, or seeds you have on hand. And sometimes the only thing you have on hand is chocolate chips, so that will do, too.

NOTE: You will need to freeze the bananas and blue berries before making this.

MAKE IT GLUTEN-FREE: Use gluten-free coconut, gluten-free chocolate chips, and gluten-free oats.

In a food processor, combine the bananas, blueberries, and almond butter. Blend until smooth (be patient, this may take a few minutes). If needed, add almond milk, 1 tablespoon at a time, to thin.

Serve in bowls topped with granola, berries, coconut, chia, and/or chocolate chips.

maple-pecan granola

MAKES 2½ CUPS

1½ cups **rolled oats**

½ cup coarsely chopped **pecans**

1 teaspoon **ground cinnamon**

⅛ teaspoon **sea salt**

¼ cup **pure maple syrup**

2 tablespoons **coconut oil**

½ teaspoon **pure vanilla extract**

½ teaspoon **pure maple extract**

Preheat the oven to 325°F. Line a baking sheet with parchment paper.

In a large bowl, stir together the oats, pecans, cinnamon, and salt. Add the maple syrup, oil, vanilla, and maple extract, and stir to coat.

Spread the mixture in an even layer on the prepared baking sheet and bake for 30 to 40 minutes, until lightly browned. Remove from the oven and let cool.

CINNAMON ROLL PANCAKES

SERVES 2

1 cup all-purpose **flour**

2 teaspoons **baking powder**

½ teaspoon **sea salt**

1 cup **almond milk**

2 tablespoons **pure maple syrup**

3 tablespoons **vegan margarine** or refined **coconut oil**, at room temperature

5 tablespoons **light brown sugar**

2 teaspoons **ground cinnamon**

Vegetable oil, for greasing

Glaze

2 cups **confectioners' sugar**

¼ cup **water**

My mom makes the best cinnamon rolls in the world. I make amazing pancakes. We have joined forces and together, we present: Cinnamon Roll Pancakes! Take one bite of this vegan brunch hybrid and you'll never need to wait in line for a Cronut again.

In a large bowl, whisk together the flour, baking powder, and salt. In a small bowl, whisk together the almond milk and maple syrup. Add the wet ingredients to the dry and whisk to combine. Do not overmix.

In a small bowl, mix together the margarine, brown sugar, and cinnamon. Transfer to a pastry bag or plastic zip-top bag and snip off one corner.

Lightly grease a large nonstick skillet or griddle and heat over medium heat. When the pan shimmers, measure out ¼ cup of the batter (or eyeball it) and pour it onto the skillet. Pipe a circular swirl of the cinnamon mixture into the batter. Repeat to fill the skillet. When small bubbles appear in the center of the pancakes, after about 4 minutes, flip. Cook on the other side for about 1 minute more, until lightly browned and cooked through. Repeat with the remaining batter, adding more oil to the skillet between batches as needed.

Meanwhile, make the glaze: in a small bowl, combine the confectioners' sugar and water and whisk until smooth.

Drizzle the pancakes with the glaze and serve.

FRENCH TOAST

SERVES 6

1 cup all-purpose **flour**

2 teaspoons **baking powder**

1 teaspoon **ground cinnamon**

1 teaspoon **ground nutmeg**

½ teaspoon **sea salt**

2 cups **almond milk**

¼ cup **pure maple syrup**, plus more for serving

3 tablespoons **vegetable oil**

2 teaspoons **pure vanilla extract**

12 to 14 slices **multigrain** or **white bread**

Confectioners' sugar, for dusting

Berries, sliced **apples**, or sliced **banana** (optional)

Quick, easy, and restaurant-quality! My boyfriend, Ben, *oohs* and *ahhs* whenever I whip this up. I always keep sliced bread of some kind stashed in my freezer, so I never have to grocery shop before making this recipe. Spontaneous French toast cravings, I'm ready for you!

In a small bowl, whisk together the flour, baking powder, cinnamon, nutmeg, and salt. In a blender or food processor, combine the almond milk, maple syrup, 2 tablespoons of the oil, and vanilla and blend until smooth. Add the dry mixture to the blender and blend again until smooth. Transfer to a large shallow bowl or baking dish.

In a large nonstick skillet or griddle, heat the remaining tablespoon of oil over medium heat. When it shimmers, working in batches as needed, submerge each piece of bread in the batter to coat, letting any excess drip off, then set the bread onto the skillet. Cook for about 3 minutes, until the bottom edges are golden. Flip and cook for about 3 minutes more, until lightly browned and crisp on both sides.

Dust the toast with confectioners' sugar and serve with fruit and warm maple syrup for dipping.

BEN'S WAFFLES WITH STRAWBERRY BUTTER

MAKES 5 WAFFLES

2 cups all-purpose **flour**

2 tablespoons **baking powder**

½ teaspoon **sea salt**

1¾ cups **almond milk**

¼ cup **pure maple syrup**, plus more for serving

2 tablespoons **pure vanilla extract**

6 tablespoons **vegetable oil**, plus more for greasing

Toppings: **Strawberry Butter** (recipe follows), **confectioners' sugar**, sliced **strawberries**, or sliced **banana** (optional)

I have always been a pancakes girl, but when my boyfriend, Ben, and I moved in together, I learned he was a waffles guy. Lucky for me, I was able to swiftly cross over to the waffle side. Lucky for him, that enabled me to create this recipe, which he loves so much. I prefer using a Belgian waffle maker, which makes a thicker waffle, but any kind will do. This recipe serves five people . . . or one Ben.

Preheat your waffle iron according to the manufacturer's instructions.

In a large bowl, whisk together the flour, baking powder, and salt. In a small bowl, whisk together the almond milk, maple syrup, vanilla, and oil. Add the wet ingredients to the dry and whisk until just combined.

Lightly grease the waffle iron and cook the waffles according to the manufacturer's instructions. Serve each waffle with a dollop of Strawberry Butter, warm maple syrup, confectioners' sugar, and/or sliced fruit.

strawberry butter

MAKES ABOUT 1¾ CUPS

1 cup **vegan margarine**

6 tablespoons **pure maple syrup**

6 **fresh strawberries**, chopped

In a food processor, combine all the ingredients and process until smooth. Store in an airtight container in the refrigerator for up to 1 week.

THE MCVEGAN BREAKFAST SANDWICH

SERVES 6

8 ounces **silken tofu**

2 tablespoons **olive** or refined **coconut oil**, plus more as needed

1 tablespoon **nutritional yeast flakes**

2 teaspoons **sea salt**

½ teaspoon **ground turmeric**

½ teaspoon **onion powder**

½ teaspoon **garlic powder**

1 small **onion**, chopped

8 ounces sliced **mushrooms**

8 ounces **ground seitan** (see Tip)

1 cup **cherry tomatoes**, halved

1 (16-ounce) package **extra-firm tofu**, drained and patted dry with paper towels

5 ounces **greens** (kale, baby spinach, or chard)

Freshly ground **black pepper**

6 **vegan English muffins** or 12 slices of **bread**, toasted

1 or 2 **avocados**, thinly sliced

Sriracha or **hot sauce** (optional)

Drive-thru breakfast, begone! This breakfast sandwich takes first prize in flavor, texture, and nutrition. Okay, I just gave that award to myself, but I promise, this recipe really does deserve it. It looks like fast food and tastes like fast food, but gives you all the energy and nourishment you need to start your day.

MAKE IT GLUTEN-FREE: Serve on gluten-free English muffins and replace the seitan with tempeh.

In a blender or food processor, combine the silken tofu, 1 tablespoon of the olive oil, nutritional yeast, salt, turmeric, onion powder, and garlic powder. Blend until smooth. If the mixture is too thick to combine, add 1 to 2 tablespoons of water and blend again as needed.

In a large nonstick skillet, heat the remaining tablespoon of olive oil over medium-high heat. When it shimmers, add the onion, mushrooms, seitan, and tomatoes and cook for 5 to 7 minutes, until onions are translucent. Using your hands, crumble the extra-firm tofu into the skillet and cook, stirring occasionally, for about 5 minutes, until lightly browned, adding more oil if needed. Add the greens and cook until just wilted, about 3 minutes. Add the pureed tofu mixture, then reduce the heat to medium and cook, stirring often, for 2 to 3 minutes, until the pureed tofu thickens. Taste and season with pepper.

Layer the bottoms of the English muffins with the scramble, sliced avocado, and a very light drizzle of sriracha, if desired. Top them with the muffin tops and serve.

TIP GROUND SEITAN

If you cannot find ground seitan, you can make your own using seitan of any shape or size (strips, cubes, etc.). Drain your seitan well, then pulse in the food processor until finely ground. Do not overpulse; the seitan should still have some texture.

HOMEMADE COCOA PUFFS

MAKES 2½ CUPS CEREAL; SERVES ABOUT 5 KIDS

½ cup whole-grain **gluten-free oat flour**

½ cup whole-grain **corn flour**

½ cup **sugar**

2 tablespoons **unsweetened, gluten-free cocoa powder**

½ teaspoon **xanthan gum**

¼ teaspoon **sea salt**

5 tablespoons **vegan margarine**

3 tablespoons very cold **water**

Nondairy milk, for serving (optional)

Cocoa Puffs were my favorite sugary breakfast cereal as a kid (I know, I know—so processed and unhealthy, it's sinful!). But somehow this vegan and gluten-free version tastes better than the real thing! Chilling the dough will make it easier to work with, but I usually get impatient and make it right away, and it still comes out okay. The most tedious part is rolling the dough into little balls. Kids are great helpers for this task, or you can even bake these off as bigger cookies instead by keeping them in the oven for a few extra minutes.

MAKE-AHEAD TIP: Cocoa Puffs can be stored in an airtight container in the freezer for up to 1 month or at room temperature for up to 5 days.

Preheat the oven to 375°F. Line a large rimmed baking sheet with parchment paper.

In a food processor, combine the oat flour, corn flour, sugar, cocoa powder, xanthan gum, and salt and pulse until combined. Add the margarine and water and process until the dough comes together.

Using your hands, roll the dough into little balls about the size of marbles, placing them on the prepared baking sheet as you work. If the dough is too sticky, chill it in the refrigerator for 30 minutes to 1 hour, until firm.

Bake for about 15 minutes, until crispy. Let cool on the pan. Serve in a bowl with nondairy milk or eat them plain.

NO-HUEVOS RANCHEROS

SERVES 4

ranchero sauce

1 (15-ounce) can whole or crushed **fire-roasted tomatoes**, with their juices

¼ cup diced **onion**

1 **garlic clove**

¼ cup coarsely chopped **fresh cilantro**, plus more for garnish

1 **jalapeño**, seeded

1 tablespoon **agave**

2 teaspoons **lime juice**

½ teaspoon **sea salt**

scramble

1 tablespoon **olive oil**, plus more as needed

¾ cup diced **onion**

1 (15-ounce) can **black beans**, drained and rinsed

1 (16-ounce) package **extra-firm tofu**, drained, patted dry, and lightly crumbled

8 ounces **ground seitan** (see Tip, page 31)

1 tablespoon **nutritional yeast flakes**

1 teaspoon **sea salt**

½ teaspoon **onion powder**

½ teaspoon **garlic powder**

½ teaspoon **taco seasoning**

¼ teaspoon **ground turmeric**

The best part about living in a doorman building in NYC is that you have a taste tester sitting in the lobby 24/7. I made this dish with my vegan roommate, Daniella, and we both went nuts for it, but we had to bring a plate down to our doorman Paul to see if it passed the test with a non-vegan. He loved it! The flavors really pop—you can't even tell you're eating tofu. While huevos rancheros is typically a brunch dish, I like to eat this for dinner, too (and so does Paul!).

MAKE-AHEAD TIP: The Ranchero Sauce and Lime Sour Cream can be made in advance, and stored in an airtight container in the refrigerator for up to 5 days.

MAKE IT GLUTEN-FREE: Replace the seitan with tempeh and use gluten-free corn tortillas.

Make the ranchero sauce: In a blender or food processor, combine the tomatoes and their juices, onion, garlic, cilantro, jalapeño, agave, lime juice, and salt and blend until smooth. Transfer to a small saucepan and warm over medium-low heat. Gently simmer until ready to serve.

Make the scramble: In a large nonstick skillet, heat the olive oil over medium-high heat. When it shimmers, add the onion and cook for 5 to 7 minutes, until softened. Add the beans, tofu, and seitan and cook for a few minutes more, until lightly browned, adding more oil if the mixture sticks to the pan. Add the nutritional yeast, salt, onion powder, garlic powder, taco seasoning, and turmeric and cook for about 1 minute more, until fragrant. Add water, 1 tablespoon at a time, if the tofu becomes dry. Reduce the heat to medium-low and add the spinach, stirring until just wilted. Taste and season with pepper.

recipe continues

3 cups (4 ounces) **baby spinach**

Freshly ground **black pepper**

to assemble

8 small soft **corn tortillas**

Lime Sour Cream (recipe follows)

1 **avocado**, sliced

To assemble, heat a tortilla in a pan over medium-high heat or by placing it directly on the burner over medium-low heat for about 20 to 30 seconds on each side, using tongs to flip. Layer a few large spoonfuls of scramble on top of the tortilla, then top with Ranchero Sauce. Drizzle with Lime Sour Cream and garnish with a few avocado slices and some cilantro. Repeat with the remaining tortillas.

lime sour cream

MAKES 1 CUP

1 cup **silken tofu**

¼ cup **olive oil**

2 tablespoons **lime juice**

½ teaspoon **sea salt**

In a blender or food processor, combine all the ingredients and blend until smooth. Store in an airtight container in the refrigerator for up to 5 days.

CHOCOLATE CHIP BANANA PANCAKES

SERVES 3

1 cup all-purpose **flour**

2 teaspoons **baking powder**

½ teaspoon **sea salt**

¼ teaspoon **ground cinnamon** (optional)

1 cup **almond milk**

1 large ripe **banana**, mashed (about ½ cup)

2 tablespoons **pure maple syrup**, plus more for serving

Vegetable oil, for the skillet

½ cup **vegan chocolate chips**

Confectioners' sugar, for dusting

Sliced **banana**, for serving (optional)

Banana is nature's miracle ingredient for vegan baking. Add it to any pastry or quick bread for an infusion of moisture and sweetness. I love these pancakes because the comforting banana bread-y aroma fills the house as they cook on the griddle—they're especially great on a snow day or cold morning. Don't forget to complete the experience with fuzzy pajamas, a roaring fire, dogs, and some Jack Johnson.

In a large bowl, whisk together the flour, baking powder, salt, and cinnamon (if using). In a medium bowl, whisk together the almond milk, banana, and maple syrup until smooth. Add the wet ingredients to the dry and whisk to combine. Do not overmix.

Lightly oil a large nonstick skillet or griddle and heat over medium heat. When the oil shimmers, measure out ¼ cup of the batter (or eyeball it) and pour it onto the skillet. Repeat to fill the skillet. Sprinkle the pancakes with chocolate chips.

When small bubbles appear in the center of the pancakes, after about 4 minutes, flip. Cook on the other side for about 1 minute more, until lightly browned and cooked through. Repeat with the remaining batter, adding more oil to the skillet between batches as needed.

Dust the pancakes with confectioners' sugar and serve with sliced bananas, if desired, and warm maple syrup.

SHELLEY'S MATZO BREI WITH HOMEMADE APPLESAUCE

SERVES 4

1 cup (8 ounces) **silken tofu**

2 tablespoons **olive** or refined **coconut oil**, plus more as needed

1 tablespoon **nutritional yeast flakes**

1½ teaspoons **sea salt**, plus more for seasoning

½ teaspoon **ground turmeric**

½ teaspoon **onion powder**

½ teaspoon **garlic powder**

½ teaspoon freshly **ground black pepper**, plus more for seasoning

4 sheets plain **matzo**

3 **scallions**, thinly sliced

About 1 cup (5 ounces) **shiitake mushrooms**, de-stemmed and thinly sliced

Confectioners' sugar, for dusting (optional)

Applesauce, store-bought or homemade (recipe follows), for serving

My Jewish mama (that's Shelley) makes the best matzo brei. It's a Passover staple, but I grew up eating it on the daily. When I went vegan, she had to find a way to keep serving me her beloved matzo brei! Sure enough, her vegan version was even better than her original. It gets topped with the best chunky applesauce—it's like eating a bowlful of the inside of an apple pie! This recipe is not kosher for Passover because tofu is not kosher for Passover; use hemp tofu to modify for Passover. Also, be sure not to use egg matzo.

MAKE IT GLUTEN-FREE: Use gluten-free matzo.

In a blender or food processor, combine the tofu, 1 tablespoon of the olive oil, nutritional yeast, salt, turmeric, onion powder, garlic powder, and pepper. Blend until smooth. If the mixture is too thick to combine, add 1 to 2 tablespoons of water.

Place the matzo in a large bowl and roughly break the sheets into quarters using your hands. Cover the matzo with water and let it soak for about 5 minutes, or until soggy, then drain.

Meanwhile, in a large nonstick skillet, heat the remaining tablespoon of olive oil over medium-high heat. When it shimmers, add the scallions and mushrooms and cook, stirring occasionally, for 6 to 8 minutes, until soft and slightly browned, adding more oil if needed. Season with salt.

recipe continues

Add the matzo and tofu mixture to the skillet. Mix with a spatula until the matzo is coated with the tofu mixture and cook for 3 to 5 minutes, until lightly browned and crispy on the edges. Season with pepper. Lightly dust with confectioners' sugar, if desired, and serve with applesauce.

applesauce

SERVES 4

 4 **apples** (I like Braeburn, Fuji, or Golden Delicious), unpeeled and diced

½ cup **apple juice**

3 tablespoons **light brown sugar**

Juice of ½ **orange**

1 teaspoon **pure vanilla extract**

½ teaspoon **ground cinnamon**

Pinch of **sea salt**

In a small saucepan, combine all the ingredients. Cook over medium heat for about 30 minutes, until the apples have broken down and softened. Let cool. Store in an airtight container in the refrigerator for up to 1 week.

SMOKY GRITS & GREENS

SERVES 4

grits

4 cups gluten-free **vegetable broth**

1 cup **grits** (not instant) or **polenta**

1½ teaspoons **smoked paprika**

¼ cup **nutritional yeast flakes**

1 tablespoon **light brown sugar**

1½ tablespoons unrefined **coconut oil**

Sea salt and freshly ground **black pepper**

greens

1 tablespoon **olive oil**

1 **garlic clove**, minced

1 bunch **greens** of choice (kale, chard, spinach, etc.), coarsely chopped

Sea salt and freshly ground **black pepper**

Both polenta and grits are made from stone-ground cornmeal, but polenta comes from Italy, whereas grits are from the southern United States. This comforting breakfast dish is my vegan take on Southern grits, but if you can't find them where you are, use polenta. The use of unrefined coconut oil imparts a slight coconutty flavor that works extremely well with the smokiness of the paprika.

Make the grits: Put the broth in a medium saucepan, cover, and bring to a boil over medium-high heat. Uncover and slowly add the grits, stirring frequently. Reduce the heat to medium-low and simmer, covered, until the grits have thickened and cooked through ("quick" grits will take about 5 minutes; polenta will take about 20 minutes). Add the smoked paprika, nutritional yeast, brown sugar, and coconut oil. Season with salt and pepper.

Meanwhile, make the greens: In a large skillet, heat the olive oil over medium-high heat. When it shimmers, add the garlic and greens and cook for 3 to 5 minutes, until the greens have wilted. Season with salt and pepper.

Spoon the grits into bowls. Top with greens and serve.

BREAKFAST SCRAMBLE WITH MAPLE SAUSAGE LINKS

SERVES 4 TO 6

1 cup (8 ounces) **silken tofu**

2 tablespoons **olive** or refined **coconut oil**

1 tablespoon **nutritional yeast flakes**

2 teaspoons **sea salt**

½ teaspoon **ground turmeric**

½ teaspoon **onion powder**

½ teaspoon **garlic powder**

3 **scallions**, thinly sliced

1½ cups (5 ounces) **shiitake mushrooms**, de-stemmed and thinly sliced

1 cup (6 ounces) **cherry tomatoes**, halved

1 (16-ounce) package **extra-firm tofu**, drained and patted dry with paper towels

3 cups (5 ounces) **greens** (kale, baby spinach, or chard)

Freshly ground **black pepper**

Maple Sausage Links (recipe follows)

Having been vegan for more than a decade, I've definitely been around the tofu scramble block. Let's just say I've eaten so many that I'm surprised I haven't turned into one by now! So take it from me that this recipe is the very best tofu scramble in all the vegan land.

In a blender or food processor, combine the silken tofu, 1 tablespoon of the olive oil, nutritional yeast, salt, turmeric, onion powder, and garlic powder. Blend until smooth. If the mixture is too thick to combine, add 1 to 2 tablespoons of water.

In a large nonstick skillet, heat the remaining tablespoon of olive oil over medium-high heat. When it shimmers, add the scallions, mushrooms, and tomatoes. Using your hands, crumble the extra-firm tofu into the skillet and sauté for 6 to 8 minutes, until the vegetables are softened and lightly browned. Add the greens and cook for about 3 minutes, until just wilted. Add the pureed tofu mixture. Reduce the heat to medium and cook, stirring often, for a few minutes more, until the pureed tofu thickens. Taste and season with pepper. Serve the scramble with the sausage links.

maple sausage links

MAKES 12 LINKS

3 tablespoons **vegetable oil**, plus more as needed

1 **onion**, finely chopped

1 (8-ounce) package **tempeh**, crumbled

2 **garlic cloves**, minced

2 teaspoons **sea salt**

¼ teaspoon **crushed red pepper flakes**

Freshly ground **black pepper**

1 (15-ounce) can **lentils**, drained and rinsed, or 1½ cups cooked lentils

¼ cup **pure maple syrup**

2 **scallions**, thinly sliced

¼ cup **bread crumbs**

MAKE-AHEAD TIP: The sausage mixture can be made ahead and stored in an airtight container in the refrigerator for up to 5 days. Or form the links and freeze for up to 2 months. When serving, panfry from frozen.

MAKE IT GLUTEN-FREE: Use gluten-free bread crumbs.

Heat 2 tablespoons of the oil in a large nonstick skillet over medium-high heat. When it shimmers, add the onion, tempeh, garlic, salt, and red pepper flakes, and season generously with black pepper. Sauté for 5 to 7 minutes, until onions are soft and tempeh is browned. Add the lentils, maple syrup, and scallions, and let cook about 2 minutes more, until heated through, tossing to coat. Transfer to a large bowl and stir in the bread crumbs until well combined, mashing up the mixture as you stir. Adjust the seasoning to taste. Let mixture sit until cool to the touch (or place in refrigerator to cool). Once cooled, use your hands to form into 3-inch links.

Heat the remaining tablespoon of oil in a large nonstick skillet over medium-high heat. When it shimmers, working in batches, add the links and pan-fry, adding more oil as needed, until very browned on all sides, turning with a spatula, about 6 minutes total. Remove the links from the pan and serve warm.

MATCHA CHOCOLATE CHIP MUFFINS

MAKES 14 MUFFINS

muffins

2 cups all-purpose **flour** or **whole-wheat pastry flour**

½ cup **granulated sugar**

1 tablespoon **matcha green tea powder**

1 tablespoon **baking powder**

½ teaspoon **sea salt**

1 cup **almond milk**

½ cup **vegetable** or refined **coconut oil**

1 teaspoon **apple cider vinegar**

2 teaspoons **pure vanilla extract**

¾ cup **vegan chocolate chips**

crumb topping

1 cup all-purpose **flour**

¼ cup **granulated sugar**

¼ cup packed **light brown sugar**

2 teaspoons **ground cinnamon**

1 teaspoon **ground nutmeg**

¼ teaspoon **sea salt**

½ cup **vegan margarine** or refined **coconut oil**, at room temperature

Confectioners' sugar, for dusting

Matcha, a specific type of green tea, has amazing health benefits: it's high in antioxidants, metabolism-boosting, and detoxifying, and it improves memory and concentration. And while I like drinking matcha, I *love* eating matcha, especially in these muffins. Sometimes I add chocolate chips to these bright-green muffins for a decadent touch—and more antioxidants, of course.

MAKE-AHEAD TIP: The crumb topping can be made in advance and stored in an airtight container in the refrigerator for up to 5 days or in the freezer for up to 1 month.

MAKE IT GLUTEN-FREE: Use gluten-free baking flour and chocolate chips.

Preheat the oven to 375°F. Line two 12-cup muffin pans with 14 liners and lightly grease the liners with cooking spray.

Make the muffins: In a large bowl, whisk together the flour, granulated sugar, matcha, baking powder, and salt. In a small bowl, whisk together the almond milk, oil, vinegar, and vanilla. Add the wet ingredients to the dry and whisk to combine. Fold in the chocolate chips.

Make the crumb topping: In a medium bowl, combine the flour, granulated sugar, brown sugar, cinnamon, nutmeg, and salt. Add the margarine and toss with two forks (like a salad) until crumbly. The lumps should be the size of small peas.

Fill the prepared muffin tins with batter, filling each cup a little more than halfway. Top each generously with 1 or 2 tablespoons of the crumb topping. Bake for about 24 minutes, until the crumb topping is golden. Let cool in the pan, them unmold and dust with confectioners' sugar.

go–withs

SNACKS
& SIDES

15-MINUTE BABA GHANOUSH

SERVES 4

2 tablespoons **olive oil**, plus more as needed

1 large **eggplant**, peeled and diced

3 **garlic cloves**

½ teaspoon **sea salt**

2 tablespoons **tahini**

1 tablespoon **lemon juice**

Pinch of **cayenne pepper**

Freshly ground **black pepper**

2 tablespoons coarsely chopped **fresh herbs** (I like flat-leaf parsley or cilantro; optional)

Smoked paprika, for dusting

Baba ghanoush is a Lebanese dip traditionally made by roasting or grilling an entire eggplant, which can often take over an hour. But in this recipe, I leave the eggplant unpeeled and sauté it, so you don't have to wrestle with roasting a whole eggplant—or wait! Serve it with raw veggies, pita, or chips for the perfect snack or appetizer.

In a large nonstick skillet, heat the olive oil over medium-high heat. When it shimmers, add the eggplant, garlic, and salt and cook, stirring frequently, for 8 to 10 minutes, until the eggplant is charred and very soft and mushy. If the eggplant looks dry, add 1 tablespoon of water at a time.

Transfer the eggplant mixture to a food processor and add the tahini, lemon juice, and cayenne. Blend until smooth, adding 1 or 2 tablespoons more olive oil as needed to achieve a creamy consistency. Season with black pepper and roughly pulse in the fresh herbs, if desired. Taste and adjust the seasoning.

Transfer to a serving plate or bowl, drizzle lightly with olive oil, and dust with smoked paprika.

ROASTED CARROT HUMMUS

SERVES 4 TO 6

3 **carrots**, cut into 1-inch pieces (about 1¼ cups)

¼ cup plus 1 teaspoon **olive oil**, plus more for drizzling

½ teaspoon plus a pinch of **sea salt**

1 (15.5-ounce) can **chickpeas**, drained and rinsed

2 tablespoons **lemon juice**

1 small **garlic clove**

Freshly ground **black pepper**

Toppings: **Pomegranate seeds**; chopped fresh **flat-leaf parsley**

Everyone likes hummus, but this version is truly loveable, crave-worthy, dream-about-it hummus. Roasting carrots at a high heat ignites a caramelization process that brings out their natural sugars. Blending this into what would otherwise be ordinary hummus adds sweetness and a bright orange color. Serve with raw veggies (anything but carrots!), pita chips, or crostini.

Preheat the oven to 400°F. Line a small rimmed baking sheet with aluminum foil.

On the prepared baking sheet, drizzle the carrots with 1 teaspoon of the olive oil and a pinch of salt. Bring the edges of the foil up and seal together, creating a pouch for the carrots. Roast for 30 minutes, until the carrots are fork-tender.

In a food processor, combine the roasted carrots, chickpeas, remaining ½ teaspoon of salt, the lemon juice, garlic, and the remaining ¼ cup of olive oil. Blend until smooth. Season with salt and pepper to taste. Top with pomegranate seeds, parsley, and a drizzle of olive oil.

CAESAR
BRUSSELS SPROUTS

SERVES 4

caesar dressing

½ cup (4 ounces) **silken tofu**, drained

⅓ cup **olive oil**

1 **garlic clove**

1 tablespoon **lemon juice**

1 tablespoon **mellow white miso paste**

1 teaspoon **Dijon mustard**

1 teaspoon **agave nectar**

½ teaspoon **sea salt**

½ teaspoon freshly ground **black pepper**

salad

2 tablespoons **olive oil**

1 pound **Brussels sprouts**, shredded (about 4 cups)

Sea salt and freshly ground **black pepper**

Chloe's Croutons (page 85)

Here I've taken the gold-standard kale Caesar and given it a twist. I chose Brussels sprouts to replace kale, because, like kale, Brussels sprouts are dense enough to carry a substantial creamy sauce like Caesar without wilting or turning soggy. To ensure the raw sprouts are not tough to chew through, I soften them slightly with a quick sauté to make them the perfect texture with just the right amount of crunch. Try this recipe and you might just give up kale forever. Kidding!

MAKE-AHEAD TIP: You can store the dressing in the refrigerator in an airtight container for up to 3 days.

MAKE IT GLUTEN-FREE: Use gluten-free mustard and omit the croutons.

Make the dressing: In a blender or food processor, combine all the dressing ingredients and blend until smooth. Set aside.

Make the salad: In a large skillet, heat the olive oil over medium-high heat. When it shimmers, add the Brussels sprouts and cook, stirring frequently, for 5 to 7 minutes, until lightly charred. Transfer the Brussels sprouts to a large bowl. Toss the sprouts with desired amount of the Caesar dressing. Adjust the seasoning to taste and top with croutons.

ARTICHOKE GARLIC BREAD

SERVES 8

About 1½ cups (12 or 16 ounces) jarred or canned **artichoke hearts**, drained

½ cup **vegan margarine**

2 tablespoons **nutritional yeast flakes**

6 **garlic cloves**, minced

½ teaspoon **sea salt**

½ cup chopped **fresh basil**

1 **baguette**

Vegan Parmesan (recipe follows)

Artichoke Basille Pizza is a popular chain in New York City whose specialty is putting spinach-artichoke dip on pizza. I've never tried it because it's not vegan, but I was certainly interested in the idea of warm, creamy artichoke on piping-hot dough. It inspired me to create this hybrid between spinach-artichoke dip and garlic bread, and I probably won't go back to regular garlic bread again. I make this whenever I'm having a large dinner party; everyone always clamors for more.

MAKE IT GLUTEN-FREE: Use gluten-free bread.

Preheat the oven to 425°F.

In a food processor, combine the artichoke hearts, margarine, nutritional yeast, garlic, and salt. Pulse until the mixture is somewhat combined but still has some texture. Add the basil and pulse again until coarsely chopped.

Slice the baguette in half horizontally and place the halves cut-side up on a baking sheet. Spread an even layer of the artichoke mixture over each half (you may not need all of it; refrigerate or freeze any leftovers for another use—or snack on it!). Sprinkle the bread with Vegan Parmesan.

Bake for about 10 minutes, until the bread turns golden, then turn the oven to broil. Broil for 1 to 2 minutes, until the edges are nicely browned, checking frequently. Keep your eyes on the bread—it can burn very quickly. Serve hot.

vegan parmesan

MAKES A HEAPING ½ CUP

½ cup blanched **almonds** or **pecans**

1 tablespoon **nutritional yeast flakes**

½ teaspoon **sea salt**

¼ teaspoon **garlic powder**

1 teaspoon **pure maple syrup** or **agave nectar**

In a food processor, combine the nuts, nutritional yeast, salt, and garlic powder. Pulse until a fine meal forms. Drizzle in the maple syrup and pulse again until incorporated. Store in an airtight container or plastic bag in the freezer for up to 6 months. (I use it straight from frozen; it thaws within seconds thanks to its fine texture!)

SWEET TAMALE CAKES

MAKES 6 CAKES

1½ cups (about 8 ounces) **frozen sweet yellow corn**, thawed

½ cup **vegan margarine**

½ cup **masa harina**

3 tablespoons all-purpose **flour**

3 tablespoons **sugar**

½ teaspoon **sea salt**

1 **jalapeño**, seeded and minced

toppings

Sriracha Mayo (page 61)

Diced **avocado**

Salsa fresca

Chopped **fresh cilantro**

These easy tamale cakes are flavorful, festive, and a perfect party appetizer! My mom and I make them for parties because they are addictively sweet and spicy, and they are much easier to eat than a full-size tamale in a husk. Masa harina is corn flour, so look for it in the baking or ethnic food aisle of your grocery store. I recommend wearing gloves to avoid skin irritation from the jalapeños, but regardless, be sure to wash your hands thoroughly before touching anything else—especially your eyes!

MAKE-AHEAD TIP: The tamale dough can be made in advance, pre-formed, and stored in an airtight container in the refrigerator for up to 5 days or in the freezer for up to 1 month. You can pan-fry directly from the refrigerator or freezer.

MAKE IT GLUTEN-FREE: Use gluten-free baking flour.

In a food processor, blend 1 cup of the corn until coarsely ground. Add the margarine, masa harina, flour, sugar, and salt and blend until a dough forms. Add the remaining ½ cup of corn and jalapeño and mix by hand. Taste and adjust the seasoning, if necessary. Scoop out ¼ cup of the dough and using your hands, form it into a patty. Repeat to make 6 patties total.

Heat a large nonstick skillet over medium heat. When the skillet is hot, working in batches if necessary, sear the patties for about 4 minutes on each side, flipping with a spatula, until lightly browned and crisp.

Serve the warm cakes with a drizzle of Sriracha Mayo and desired toppings.

CHARRED CHILI-LIME STREET CORN

SERVES 4

1 tablespoon **vegetable oil**

3 cups (1 pound) **frozen sweet yellow corn**

1 **jalapeño**, seeded and minced

1 teaspoon **sea salt**

2 teaspoons fresh **lime juice**

1 teaspoon **agave nectar**

1 tablespoon **vegan margarine**

toppings

Smoked paprika

Chopped **fresh cilantro**

Lime wedge

Sriracha Mayo (recipe follows)

Corn is a popular street food in Mexico, often slathered with various forms of cheese. This vegan version has just as much going on, from the juicy sweet corn to the fresh lime to the smoky paprika and creamy sriracha mayo. It's one of those side dishes that leaves you wanting more and more and more. And it pairs so well with burgers or tacos!

In a large skillet, heat the oil over medium-high heat. When it shimmers, add the corn, jalapeño, and salt and cook, stirring frequently, for 8 to 10 minutes, until the corn is nicely charred. Stir in the lime juice, agave, and margarine. Taste and adjust the seasoning.

Portion into small bowls or cups and top with smoked paprika, cilantro, and a lime wedge. Drizzle with Sriracha Mayo.

sriracha mayo

MAKES ABOUT 1 CUP

1 cup (8 ounces) **silken tofu** or **vegan mayonnaise**

2 tablespoons **ketchup**

2 tablespoons **agave**

2 tablespoons **sriracha**

1 teaspoon **salt**

In a blender or food processor, combine all the ingredients and blend until smooth. Store in an airtight container in the refrigerator for up to 5 days.

APRICOT-SESAME CAULIFLOWER WINGS

SERVES 4

glaze

4 ounces **apricot jam**

1½ tablespoons **sriracha**

¼ cup **water**

1 teaspoon minced **fresh ginger**

1 **garlic clove**, minced or crushed

1 tablespoon **ketchup**

cauliflower

1 small head **cauliflower**, cut into 1-inch florets

1 cup **rice flour**

1½ cups all-purpose **flour**

1 tablespoon **baking powder**

1 teaspoon **garlic powder**

1 teaspoon **onion powder**

½ teaspoon **paprika**

½ teaspoon **chili powder**

½ teaspoon **cayenne pepper**

2 teaspoons **sea salt**

Freshly ground **black pepper**

2 tablespoons **sesame oil**

2 cups ice-cold **seltzer water**, plus ¼ cup or more, if needed

Vegetable oil, for frying

Sesame seeds, for garnish

Thinly sliced **scallions**, for garnish

This is my go-to appetizer recipe for Super Bowl parties, potlucks, or game nights, and my friends and family request it all the time now. It's kind of like a fusion of Buffalo chicken wings and orange chicken, so it's a mega crowd-pleaser. If you don't like sweet food, this might not be the app for you. I, on the other hand, would prefer that all my savory food borders on the dessert cutoff, so I'm pretty much addicted to the sweet, sticky glaze that coats these wings.

MAKE-AHEAD TIP: The glaze can be made ahead and stored in the refrigerator for up to 5 days.

Make the glaze: In a small saucepan, combine all the glaze ingredients. Whisk over medium heat for 3 to 5 minutes, until just boiling and thickened. Remove the pot from the heat and set aside to cool.

Make the cauliflower: Fill a large bowl with ice and tap water. Bring a large pot of salted water to a boil over high heat. Blanch the florets for 1 minute, then submerge them in the ice water. Drain the cauliflower and pat dry. In a large bowl, toss the blanched cauliflower with ½ cup of the rice flour and season generously with salt. Shake off the excess flour and set aside.

In a large bowl, whisk together the all-purpose flour, remaining ½ cup of rice flour, the baking powder, garlic powder, onion powder, paprika, chili powder, cayenne, and salt. Season with black pepper. In a small bowl, whisk together the sesame oil and seltzer water. Add the wet ingredients to the dry and whisk until it forms a thin batter—some lumps are okay. Place the batter in the refrigerator until ready to fry.

Fill a deep high-sided heavy skillet with about 3 inches of vegetable oil. Heat the oil to 350°F, or until a small drop of batter sizzles when added.

One piece at a time, dip the cauliflower into the batter, letting any excess drip off. Working in batches so as not to crowd the pan, gently place the cauliflower in the oil—the oil should sizzle. Fry for 45 seconds to 1 minute, turning halfway through, until crispy and lightly browned on the outside. Drain on paper towels. Let the oil return to 350°F between batches.

In a large bowl, toss the fried cauliflower with as much glaze as needed. Garnish with sesame seeds and scallions and serve.

GOLDFISH CRACKERS

MAKES ABOUT 10 DOZEN CRACKERS

1 cup all-purpose **flour**, plus more for dusting

2 tablespoons **nutritional yeast flakes**

1 teaspoon **sea salt**

¼ teaspoon **onion powder**

⅛ teaspoon **ground turmeric**

½ teaspoon freshly ground **black pepper** (optional)

5 tablespoons **vegan margarine**

3 tablespoons very cold tap **water**

One fish, two fish, kids *love* these all-natural homemade Goldfish. If we're being honest, adults love them, too. Am I right? I've made these for eight-year-olds and eighty-year-olds, and the response is always the same: More, please! No artificial food coloring, no sugar, no cheese, no artificial anything—just wholesome, delicious fishies. I like to add a dash of black pepper for a little spice, but some kids prefer them without. You can purchase a mini fish cookie cutter online, but frankly, they're delicious no matter the shape.

MAKE IT GLUTEN-FREE: Use gluten-free baking flour.

Preheat the oven to 375°F.

In a food processor, combine the flour, nutritional yeast, salt, onion powder, turmeric, and pepper (if using). Pulse until combined. Add the margarine and pulse about 15 times, until crumbly. Add the water and process until the mixture just comes together to form a dough.

On a lightly floured work surface, roll out the dough until it is ⅛ inch thick—it will be easier to roll if you work with half the dough at a time. Using a mini fish or other small cookie cutter, cut out the dough and place the shapes on a large baking sheet. If desired, use the tine of a fork or a toothpick to carve a face into your fish.

Bake for 12 to 15 minutes, until golden and very lightly browned. Let cool. Store at room temperature in a tightly sealed container or bag for up to 1 week.

CRUNCHY SNACKING CHICKPEAS

MAKES ¾ CUP; SERVES 2 AS A SNACK

1 (15.5-ounce) can **chickpeas**, drained and rinsed

2 tablespoons **olive oil**

¾ teaspoon **sea salt**

½ teaspoon **dried basil**

½ teaspoon **dried thyme**

Freshly ground **black pepper**

This is a great lunchbox snack, salad topping, or post-yoga protein source. I always make these chickpeas with plans to snack on them throughout the week, but usually end up finishing the entire batch straight from the oven. Feel free to play around with the spices to find exactly what you like best. A pinch of cayenne can turn these into flamin'-hot chickpeas!

Preheat the oven to 400°F.

Thoroughly dry the chickpeas by patting them with a paper towel or kitchen towel. Transfer to a large rimmed baking sheet. Add the olive oil, salt, basil, and thyme and season with pepper. Toss to coat evenly and arrange in an even layer.

Roast for about 45 minutes, gently turning with a spatula two or three times, until crisp. Store in an airtight container at room temperature for up to 3 days.

OVEN FRIES WITH ROASTED BEET-GINGER KETCHUP

SERVES 2

1 **russet potato**, cut into ½-inch-thick fries and patted dry with paper towels

2 tablespoons **olive** or **vegetable oil**

½ teaspoon **paprika**

½ teaspoon **onion powder**

½ teaspoon **garlic powder**

½ teaspoon **sea salt**

Roasted Beet-Ginger Ketchup (recipe follows)

What's prettier than red ketchup? Fuchsia ketchup! I created this recipe because I was bored with the color of the store-bought stuff and wanted to make things interesting. You could dip anything into this bright, sweet, tangy deliciousness. It pairs great with homemade fries; together these elements refresh that comforting combo we all know and love.

Preheat the oven to 400°F.

On a rimmed baking sheet, toss the potatoes with the olive oil, paprika, onion powder, garlic powder, and salt. Spread them into a single layer, spacing them apart. Bake for 30 to 40 minutes, until the edges are crisp, turning occasionally with a spatula. Serve with the ketchup alongside.

roasted beet-ginger ketchup

MAKES ABOUT ¾ CUP

2 tablespoons **olive oil**

2 large **shallots**, roughly chopped

½ teaspoon **sea salt**

2 ounces (scant ⅓ cup) **roasted beets** (see Tip, page 12)

3 tablespoons **pure maple syrup**

3 tablespoons **seasoned rice vinegar**

1 teaspoon minced **fresh ginger**

In a small skillet, heat the olive oil over medium heat. Add the shallots and salt and cook, stirring occasionally, for about 10 minutes, until very soft and caramelized.

Transfer the shallots to a blender and add the beets, maple syrup, vinegar, and ginger. Blend until smooth. Serve immediately or store in an airtight container in the refrigerator for up to 1 week.

GARLIC SMASHED POTATOES

SERVES 6

1½ pounds (24 ounces) **baby yellow potatoes** (bite-size, or as small as you can find them)

3 tablespoons **olive oil**

3 **garlic cloves**, minced or crushed

Sea salt and freshly ground **black pepper**

Chopped **fresh flat-leaf parsley**, for garnish

Looking for a French-fry upgrade? These crispy, salty, garlicky potato bites are elegant yet finger-licking addicting. Besides being delicious to eat, they are also extra fun to make. You smash them one by one to create flattened crispy edges, which is surprisingly therapeutic and stress-relieving!

Preheat the oven to 450°F.

Bring a large pot of heavily salted water to a boil over high heat. Add the potatoes. Cook for about 15 minutes, until fork-tender, then drain well.

Transfer the potatoes to a large rimmed baking sheet and pat dry. Toss with the olive oil and garlic and generously season with salt and pepper. Using the back of a spoon, fork, or measuring cup, firmly smash each potato once so that it is flattened but still holds together in one piece.

Bake for 15 to 20 minutes, or until the edges are crispy. Check once during baking; if the potatoes look too dry, add more oil. Taste and adjust the seasoning; garnish with parsley.

MISO CREAMED KALE

SERVES 4

½ cup **raw cashews** (see Tip, page 11)

½ cup **water**

1 tablespoon **mellow white miso paste**

½ teaspoon **sea salt**

1 tablespoon **olive oil**, plus more as needed

1 small **onion**, finely chopped

2 **garlic cloves**, minced

1 bunch **kale**, de-stemmed, leaves chopped very finely (about 4 cups)

Pinch of **ground nutmeg**

Freshly ground **black pepper**

Creamed spinach is delicious, but predictable. Creamed kale? Surprise! This dish is next-level. The luscious creamy miso sauce coats the kale decadently, making this the perfect veggie side for a Thanksgiving table or winter night.

In a blender, combine the cashews, water, miso, and salt and blend on high speed for at least 1 full minute, until the mixture is very smooth.

In a large skillet, heat the olive oil over medium-high heat. When it shimmers, add the onion and cook, stirring occasionally, for 5 to 7 minutes, until soft. Stir in the garlic. Working in batches, add the kale and cook for 5 to 7 minutes, until wilted, adding more oil as needed if the pan looks dry.

Add the cashew cream and cook for about 3 minutes, until heated through. Season with the nutmeg and pepper to taste. Taste and adjust the seasoning before serving.

PUMPKIN-SWIRL MASHED POTATOES

SERVES 4 TO 6

1 (14-ounce) can **pure pumpkin puree**

¼ cup packed **light brown sugar**

3 **russet potatoes** (about 1½ pounds), peeled and roughly chopped

½ cup **almond milk** or **vegetable broth**, plus more as needed

3 tablespoons **vegan margarine** or **olive oil**, plus more as needed

Sea salt and freshly ground **black pepper**

Country Gravy (page 180; optional)

Luscious, lofty mashed potatoes swirled with a buttery, golden ribbon of pumpkin puree and a river of creamy gravy make for the perfect treat for your eyes and palate! This recipe can also be found in *Cherry Bombe: The Cookbook* written by my food-loving sisters Kerry Diamond and Claudia Wu. I shared it with them because it's a recipe that's near and dear to my heart. My mom and I made this side dish and nine other courses when we catered my brother's vegan wedding together, and believe it or not, these taters garnered all the praise—even more than the cake!

In a medium bowl, combine the pumpkin puree and brown sugar.

Place the potatoes in a large pot and cover with heavily salted water. Cover and bring to a boil over high heat. Boil the potatoes about 15 minutes, until fork-tender. Drain the potatoes and return them to the pot, off the heat.

Add the almond milk and margarine to the pot and mash everything together. Add more almond milk or margarine as needed, until the desired consistency is reached. Season generously with salt and pepper.

Swirl in the pumpkin mixture, stirring gently and being careful not to combine completely. Cover the pot (still off the heat) for about 5 minutes to rewarm the pumpkin swirl. Serve with Country Gravy, if desired.

SCALLION PANCAKES

SERVES 6

pancakes

1 cup all-purpose **flour**

1 teaspoon **baking powder**

½ teaspoon **sea salt**

1 cup **water**

2 teaspoons **toasted sesame oil**, plus more for greasing

3 **scallions**, thinly sliced, plus more for garnish

avocado salsa

2 **avocados**, diced

2 teaspoons **lemon** or **lime juice**

Sea salt and freshly ground **black pepper**

Optional toppings: Quartered **cherry tomatoes**; **black sesame seeds**

I love ordering scallion pancakes in Chinese restaurants but I'm always discouraged from making them at home because they are labor-intensive and require a rolling pin. This batter doesn't require any rolling and still has that crispy-on-the-outside, soft-on-the-inside texture. I like to top them with avocado salsa, which adds a cool and creamy element to this decadent appetizer.

Make the pancakes: In a large bowl, whisk together the flour, baking powder, and salt. Add the water and sesame oil and whisk thoroughly until smooth. Fold in the scallions and set the batter aside for about 5 minutes to thicken.

Lightly oil a large nonstick skillet or griddle and heat over medium-high heat. When the oil shimmers, pour a few tablespoons of the batter onto the skillet to make a pancake. Repeat to fill the skillet with pancakes. When small bubbles appear in the centers of the pancakes, flip them, cooking for about 3 minutes on each side, until lightly browned and cooked through. Repeat with the remaining batter, adding more oil to the skillet between batches as needed.

Make the avocado salsa: In a medium bowl, toss together the avocado, lemon juice, and salt and pepper to taste.

Serve a spoonful of the avocado salsa on top of each pancake and season again with salt and pepper. Garnish with cherry tomatoes and black sesame seeds as desired.

SWEET POTATO CASSEROLE

SERVES 6 TO 8

3 large **garnet yams** (about 1½ pounds), peeled and roughly chopped

pecan streusel

2 tablespoons all-purpose **flour**

½ cup **pecans**

¼ cup packed **light brown sugar**

2 teaspoons **ground cinnamon**

¼ teaspoon **ground nutmeg**

Pinch of **sea salt**

1½ tablespoons **vegetable oil**

casserole

1 cup canned **coconut milk**, mixed well (see Tip, page 15)

⅓ cup packed **light brown sugar**

½ teaspoon **sea salt**

¼ teaspoon **ground cinnamon**, plus more for dusting

¼ teaspoon **ground cloves**

¼ teaspoon **ground ginger**

1 teaspoon **pure vanilla extract**

⅓ cup sweetened **dried cranberries**

½ cup **vegan marshmallows** (see page 17)

I made this dish for a Thanksgiving episode of NBC's *Today* show and the response was two thumbs up from all the anchors and staff. Whether it counts as dinner or dessert is debatable, because on one hand, it's sweet potato (a vegetable!), but on the other hand, it has an ooey-gooey marshmallow top. What's the point of Thanksgiving if not to blur that line?

MAKE-AHEAD TIP: You can assemble the entire dish up to 2 days in advance. Store, covered, in the refrigerator and bake before serving.

MAKE IT GLUTEN-FREE: Use gluten-free baking flour in the streusel and gluten-free marshmallows.

Preheat the oven to 400°F. Lightly grease an 8-inch square pan with cooking spray.

Place the yams in a large pot and cover with water. Cover and bring to a boil over high heat. Cook for 15 to 20 minutes, until fork-tender. Drain the yams and return to the pot.

Meanwhile, make the pecan streusel: In a food processor, combine the flour, pecans, brown sugar, cinnamon, nutmeg, and salt and pulse until crumbly. Add the oil and pulse until crumbly and somewhat combined.

Make the casserole: Add the coconut milk, brown sugar, salt, cinnamon, cloves, ginger, and vanilla to the yams. Mash with a potato masher until you achieve a chunky texture. Taste and adjust the seasoning. Stir in the cranberries. Transfer to the prepared pan. Top with the streusel and marshmallows.

Bake for 15 to 20 minutes, until the marshmallows are toasted. Dust with cinnamon and serve.

AVOCADO-PEACH BRUSCHETTA

SERVES 6 TO 8

1 **avocado**, diced

1 **peach**, diced

½ cup chopped **fresh basil**

1 tablespoon **white balsamic vinegar**

1 tablespoon **olive oil**, plus more for drizzling

1 teaspoon **agave**

¼ teaspoon **sea salt**

¼ teaspoon freshly ground **black pepper**

1 small **French baguette**, cut on an angle into ½-inch-thick slices

Balsamic glaze, for drizzling

This summer appetizer has a ton of flavor and color and juices! The sweet and tangy peaches pair nicely with the creamy avocado—they're the perfect foil for each other. It's a delicious way to freshen up your backyard BBQ.

MAKE IT GLUTEN-FREE: Use gluten-free bread.

Preheat the oven to 425°F.

In a large bowl, lightly toss together the avocado, peach, basil, vinegar, olive oil, agave, salt, and pepper. Set aside to let the flavors come together while you toast the bread.

Place the bread slices on a large rimmed baking sheet and drizzle lightly with olive oil. Bake for 5 to 8 minutes, until lightly browned on top.

Place the bread on a platter, top each slice with the avocado-peach mixture, and drizzle with balsamic glaze.

THAI TOFU SATAY
SERVES 4

peanut sauce

½ cup **creamy peanut butter**

¼ cup **pure maple syrup**

¼ cup **lime juice**

1 tablespoon **tamari**

1 tablespoon **sriracha**

2 teaspoons minced **fresh ginger**

1 **garlic clove**, minced

tofu

2 tablespoons **vegetable oil**, plus more as needed

1 (16-ounce) package **extra-firm tofu**, pressed (see Tip, page 14) and cut into 1-inch cubes

1 tablespoon **tamari**

2 tablespoons **pure maple syrup**

1 tablespoon **lime juice**

1 teaspoon **ground turmeric**

1 teaspoon **sriracha**

Lime wedges, for serving

optional garnishes

White or black **sesame seeds**

Chopped **fresh cilantro**

Crushed **peanuts**

Why does food taste so much better when it's served on a skewer? I think it's because it adds a little drama to the plate and immediately looks more professional than your ordinary home-cooked dish. This is my vegan take on chicken satay—still sweet, tangy, and full of flavor! Any leftover peanut sauce can be used on rice or veggies.

MAKE-AHEAD TIP: The peanut sauce can be made in advance and stored in an airtight container in the refrigerator for up to 5 days.

MAKE IT GLUTEN-FREE: Use gluten-free tamari.

Make the peanut sauce: In a food processor, combine all the peanut sauce ingredients and blend until smooth. Transfer to a few small dishes for dipping and set aside.

Make the tofu: In a large nonstick skillet, heat the oil over medium-high heat. When it shimmers, working in batches, add the tofu and sear for 2 to 3 minutes per side, until golden and crispy, using a spatula or tongs to rotate the tofu so that all sides are cooked. Add more oil as needed between batches.

Meanwhile, whisk together the tamari, maple syrup, lime juice, turmeric, and sriracha in a small bowl. Add all the seared tofu to the pan if it's not there already, then add the tamari mixture, stir to coat, and cook for about 3 minutes more to warm through.

Turn off the heat and thread the tofu cubes onto skewers. Serve with the peanut sauce, lime wedges, and optional garnishes.

TOMATO TOAST

SERVES 6 TO 8

6 **garlic cloves**

1 (28-ounce) can whole peeled **tomatoes**, drained

1 large **French baguette**, halved horizontally

Olive oil, for drizzling

Coarse or flaky **sea salt**

Freshly ground **black pepper**

Pan con tomate is a simple Spanish tapa that consists of bread, olive oil, garlic, tomato, and salt. Instead of peeling and grating tomatoes as the dish is traditionally prepared, I like to use canned whole peeled tomatoes (preferably San Marzano) as a shortcut. If you have extra tomato mixture, store it for another use in an airtight container in the refrigerator for up to 1 week.

MAKE IT GLUTEN-FREE: Use gluten-free bread.

Preheat the oven to 425°F.

In a food processor, pulse the garlic until finely chopped. Scrape down the sides with a rubber spatula and add the tomatoes. Blend until combined.

Place the baguette cut-side up on a baking sheet. Drizzle the bread with olive oil. Bake for 6 to 8 minutes, until golden. Remove the toast from the oven and turn the oven to broil.

Spread a layer of the tomato mixture on top of the bread and season with salt and pepper. Broil for a minute or two, checking frequently, until the edges are nicely browned. Keep your eyes on the bread—depending on the strength of your oven, it can burn very quickly!

Remove from the oven and drizzle again with olive oil. Serve warm.

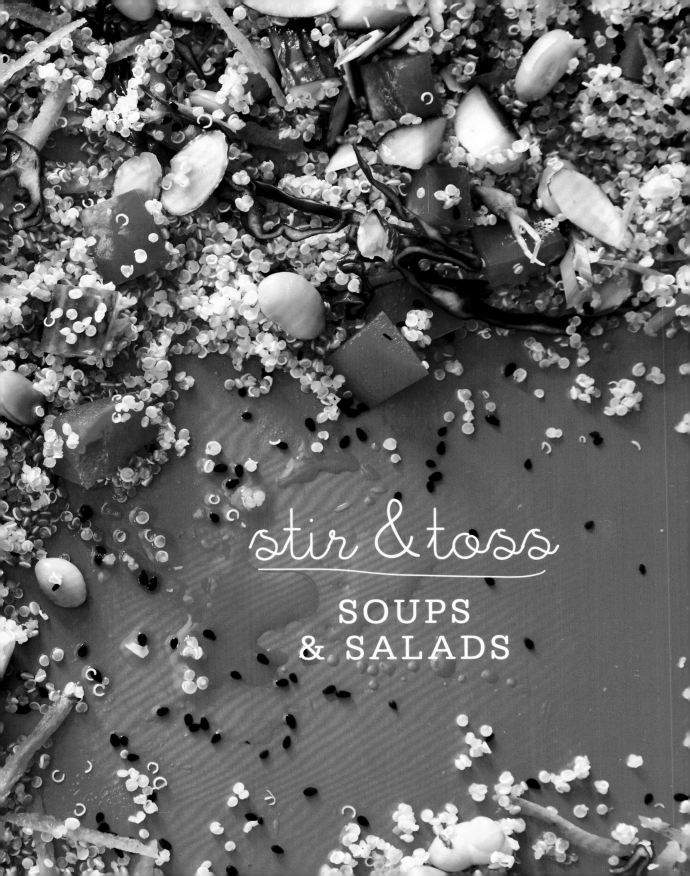

stir & toss

SOUPS
& SALADS

HEALING CREAM OF GREENS SOUP

SERVES 4 TO 6

2 tablespoons unrefined **coconut oil**

1 **onion**, diced

1 **sweet apple** such as Gala, Honeycrisp, or Braeburn, diced

4 **garlic cloves**

2 teaspoons **sea salt**

5 cups (1 pound) **frozen broccoli florets**

3 cups (5 ounces) **baby spinach**

4 cups gluten-free **vegetable broth**

Freshly ground **black pepper**

This is the perfect soup to make when you feel like you're getting sick, because the greens are packed with phytonutrients and antioxidants. I love the super-subtle coconutty notes from the unrefined coconut oil, but if you don't have any you could use olive oil instead. To add even more nourishing ingredients, try ginger or cayenne to kick up the heat and clear your sinuses. Stir in some cooked quinoa for a heartier meal.

In a large saucepan, heat 1 tablespoon of the coconut oil over medium-high heat. When it shimmers, add the onion, apple, garlic, and 1 teaspoon of the salt. Cook, stirring occasionally, for 5 to 7 minutes, until the vegetables have softened.

Add the broccoli, spinach, broth, and remaining teaspoon of the salt. Bring to a boil, then reduce the heat to medium-low and simmer for about 10 minutes, until the broccoli is tender and the spinach has wilted.

Remove the pot from the heat and puree directly in the pot using an immersion blender, or, working in batches, transfer the mixture to a blender and puree until smooth (be careful when blending hot liquids); return the soup to the pot. Stir in the remaining tablespoon of oil.

Serve in bowls topped with some pepper.

CHIPOTLE SWEET POTATO–KALE SOUP

SERVES 4

1 tablespoon **olive oil**

1 **onion**, coarsely chopped

2 **garlic cloves**, minced

1½ teaspoons **sea salt**

1 teaspoon **curry powder**

¼ teaspoon **cayenne pepper**

¼ teaspoon **chipotle powder**

2½ cups **vegetable broth**

1 cup mashed cooked **sweet potato** (about 1 medium sweet potato)

2 cups (about 4½ ounces) chopped **kale leaves**

1 cup canned **coconut milk**, plus more for drizzling (see Tip, page 15)

2 tablespoons **light brown sugar**

Chloe's Croutons (recipe follows; optional)

This soup is addicting—you can't have just one bowl! It's sweet and creamy with a kick of chipotle and cayenne. The sweet potato can be baked, boiled, or microwaved, and you can feel free to swap out the kale for any other greens you love (like collards, spinach, or chard). Make this soup your own and share your version of the recipe!

MAKE IT GLUTEN-FREE: Use gluten-free broth and if serving with croutons, make them gluten-free.

In a large saucepan, heat the olive oil over medium-high heat. When it shimmers, add the onion and cook, stirring occasionally, for 5 to 7 minutes, until softened. Add the garlic, salt, curry powder, cayenne, and chipotle powder and cook for about 1 minute more, until fragrant. Add the broth and sweet potato and bring to a boil.

Remove the pot from the heat and puree directly in the pot using an immersion blender, or, working in batches, transfer the soup to a blender and puree until smooth (be careful when blending hot liquids); return the soup to the pot. Add the kale and cook over medium heat for about 3 minutes, until wilted. Stir in the coconut milk and brown sugar. Taste and adjust the seasoning. Serve warm, topped with croutons, if desired.

chloe's croutons

MAKES 3 CUPS

3 tablespoons **olive oil**, plus more as needed

3 cups cubed or torn **bread**

Sea salt and freshly ground **black pepper**

½ teaspoon **garlic powder**

MAKE IT GLUTEN-FREE: Use gluten-free bread.

In a large skillet, heat the olive oil over medium-high heat. When it shimmers, add the bread and cook for about 5 minutes, stirring frequently, until lightly toasted. Season with salt and pepper. Add more oil if the pan looks dry.

Turn off the heat and toss with the garlic powder. Serve warm or at room temperature. Store in an airtight container at room temperature for up to 1 week or in the freezer for up to 1 month.

STONE FRUIT CAPRESE SALAD

SERVES 4

2 **stone fruits**, pitted and cut into 1-inch pieces

1 cup (5 ounces) **cherry tomatoes**, halved

1 cup (1 ounce) **arugula**

½ cup torn **basil** leaves, plus whole leaves for garnish

1 tablespoon **olive oil**

1 tablespoon **balsamic vinegar**

Sea salt and freshly ground **black pepper**

1 **avocado**, diced

¼ cup crumbled **extra-firm tofu** (optional)

Stone fruit is any fruit with a pit (peaches, nectarines, plums, and apricots, to name a few). The key to this fresh summer salad is to keep the pieces of fruit, avocado, and tofu on the larger side, so that, as with any good caprese salad, you can really taste the individual ingredients. While traditional caprese pairs tomato and mozzarella, the addition of stone fruit adds bursts of juicy sweetness that totally distract from the fact that you've subbed in tofu for cheese!

NOTE: Since the recipe only calls for 1 cup of arugula, sometimes I'll just grab that at the salad bar section of the grocery store instead of buying a whole bag of it.

In a large bowl, combine the fruit, cherry tomatoes, arugula, basil, olive oil, and vinegar. Toss to combine and season with salt and pepper. Add the avocado and top with tofu, if desired. Garnish with whole basil leaves and serve.

BUTTERNUT BISQUE

SERVES 4 TO 6

1½ pounds (24 ounces) cubed **butternut squash**

4 tablespoons **olive oil**

2 teaspoons **sea salt**

Freshly ground **black pepper**

1 **onion**, coarsely chopped

1 **apple**, peeled and sliced

1 **garlic clove**, minced

½ teaspoon **dried rosemary**

⅛ teaspoon **cayenne pepper**

4 cups gluten-free **vegetable broth**

¾ cup canned **coconut milk**, mixed well (see Tip, page 15), plus more for drizzling

One year when I was a kid, we took a family vacation to New York City for Thanksgiving. For the first time, we ate in a restaurant for Thanksgiving dinner, and I remember being served butternut squash bisque. My mind was blown because a) who knew you could eat in a restaurant for Thanksgiving? And b) the soup was so silky and luscious, it blew my mind. While the concept of butternut squash bisque may not be quite as novel as it was twenty years ago, it is still super tasty and should be in everyone's recipe arsenal.

Preheat the oven to 425°F.

On a large rimmed baking sheet, toss the squash with 2 tablespoons of the olive oil and ½ teaspoon of the salt. Season with black pepper. Roast for 30 to 40 minutes, until fork-tender.

In a large saucepan, heat the remaining 2 tablespoons of olive oil over medium-high heat. When it shimmers, add the onion and apple and cook, stirring occasionally, for about 10 minutes, until softened. Add the garlic, remaining 1½ teaspoons of salt, the rosemary, and the cayenne and cook for about 1 minute more, until fragrant. Add the broth and roasted butternut squash and bring to a boil.

Remove the pot from heat and puree directly in the pot using an immersion blender, or, working in batches, transfer the soup to a blender and puree until very smooth (be careful when blending hot liquids); return the soup to the pot.

Stir in the coconut milk, taste, and adjust the seasoning. Serve in bowls, garnished with a drizzle of coconut milk.

MEXICAN CAESAR SALAD

SERVES 4

mexican caesar dressing

½ cup (4 ounces) **silken tofu**, drained

⅓ cup **olive** or **vegetable oil**

1 **garlic clove**, minced

2 tablespoons **lime juice**

1 teaspoon **Dijon mustard**

2 teaspoons **agave nectar**

1 teaspoon **sea salt**

½ teaspoon freshly ground **black pepper**

1 **jalapeño**, seeded and chopped

¼ cup chopped **fresh cilantro**

3 **scallions**, white and light green parts only, roughly chopped

salad

About 4 cups (12 ounces) chopped **romaine** or finely chopped **kale leaves**

½ cup halved **cherry tomatoes**

1 **avocado**, diced

1 **scallion**, thinly sliced

1 **ear of fresh corn**, shucked, or ½ cup thawed **frozen corn kernels**

Sea salt and freshly ground **black pepper**

Chloe's Croutons (page 85; optional)

Vegan Caesar dressing with a kick of jalapeño, cilantro, and scallions? Heck, yes! It's kind of like Caesar salad meets guacamole (two of my most favorite foods!). The dressing is ultra-creamy and packed with flavor—I usually start eating it with a spoon before the other components of my salad are ready. You could also use it as a dip for raw veggies, drizzle it over rice or quinoa, or just bathe in it.

MAKE-AHEAD TIP: The dressing can be made in advance and stored in an airtight container in the refrigerator for up to 3 days.

MAKE IT GLUTEN-FREE: Use gluten-free mustard and, if serving with croutons, make them gluten-free.

Make the dressing: In a food processor, combine the tofu, olive oil, garlic, lime juice, mustard, agave, salt, and pepper and process until smooth. Add the jalapeño, cilantro, and scallions and process until the mixture is almost combined with some specks of green remaining.

Make the salad: In a large bowl, combine the lettuce, tomatoes, avocado, scallion, and corn. Add dressing as desired and toss to coat. Season with salt and pepper and top with some croutons, if desired.

POTATO LEEK SOUP

SERVES 6

1 tablespoon **olive oil**

2 large **leeks**, thinly sliced (see Tip, below)

6 **garlic cloves**, minced

1 teaspoon **sea salt**

½ teaspoon **dried thyme**

3 large **Yukon Gold** or **yellow potatoes** (2 to 2½ pounds), peeled and cut into bite-size pieces

Freshly ground **black pepper**

4 cups **vegetable broth**

Toppings: Chopped **chives**; **smoked paprika**; **Chloe's Croutons** (page 85; optional)

This is the kind of creamy, comforting soup that I make on days when I don't feel like leaving my apartment, it's snowing outside, and/or eating salad sounds terrible. It's the soup that nourishes my soul, and I hope it nourishes yours, too!

MAKE IT GLUTEN-FREE: Use gluten-free broth and if serving with croutons, make them gluten-free.

In a large saucepan, heat the olive oil over medium-high heat. When it shimmers, add the leeks and cook, stirring occasionally, for 5 to 7 minutes, until softened. Add the garlic, salt, thyme, and potatoes and season generously with pepper. Cook for about 1 minute more, until fragrant. Add the broth and bring to a boil, then reduce the heat and simmer for about 10 minutes, until the potatoes are very soft.

Transfer about half the mixture to a blender and puree until smooth (be careful when blending hot liquids); return the pureed soup to the pot. (Alternatively, use an immersion blender to partially blend the soup directly in the pot.) Stir so that the overall consistency of the soup is creamy but chunky. If the soup is too thick, add water a tablespoon at a time to thin it.

Taste and adjust the seasoning. Ladle into bowls, top each serving with chives, and dust with smoked paprika. Serve with croutons, if desired.

TIP CLEANING LEEKS

Leeks can be very sandy, so they need to be cleaned well before using. First, rinse them and cut off the dark green leaves and the root, leaving only the white and light green parts. Slice the stalk in half lengthwise. Lay the leek halves on your cutting surface with the flat sides down and thinly slice them crosswise into half-moons. Place the leeks in a colander or strainer in a large bowl and add enough cold water to cover them. Let the leeks soak, swishing the water a few times to loosen the sand between the layers of the leeks. The sand will sink to the bottom of the bowl. Lift the colander out of the water, being careful not to disturb the grit on the bottom of the bowl, and dry them.

FIESTA TACO BOWL

SERVES 4

green goddess dressing

⅓ cup **olive oil**

¼ cup **lime juice**

½ cup chopped **fresh cilantro**

2 tablespoons **agave nectar**

1 **jalapeño**, seeded

¼ teaspoon **sea salt**

¼ teaspoon freshly ground **black pepper**

smoky seitan

2 tablespoons **olive oil**

8 ounces **ground seitan** (see Tip, page 31)

1 teaspoon **chili powder**

1 teaspoon **smoked paprika**

Pinch of **cayenne pepper**

Sea salt

2 heads (about 15 ounces) **romaine lettuce**, cut or torn into bite-size pieces

1 cup cooked **quinoa**

1 cup canned **black beans**, drained and rinsed

1 cup (6 ounces) **frozen sweet yellow corn**, thawed

1 cup (5 ounces) halved **cherry tomatoes**

1 **avocado**, mashed

Crispy Tortilla Strips (page 101; optional)

Lime Sour Cream (page 36)

Lime wedges, for serving

Despite the stereotypical public opinion of what vegans eat, I actually don't consider myself to be much of a salad person. Leaves and veggies don't count as lunch to me, so in order for a salad to satisfy me, it needs to be super hearty, with interesting textures and flavors. This recipe is kind of like a hybrid between a bowl and a salad because it has just the right balance between fresh raw veggies and warm, spiced cooked components. Finally, a salad that knocks my little vegan socks off! The dressing isn't your typical green goddess because it is lighter, tangier, and more refreshing than the traditional dairy-based recipe.

MAKE-AHEAD TIP: The dressing can be made in advance and stored in an airtight container in the refrigerator for up to 3 days.

MAKE IT GLUTEN-FREE: Replace the seitan with tempeh and make sure the tortilla chips are gluten-free.

Make the green goddess dressing: Combine all the dressing ingredients in a blender or food processor and blend until smooth. Set aside.

Make the smoky seitan: In a large skillet, heat the olive oil over medium heat. When it shimmers, add the seitan, chili powder, smoked paprika, and cayenne and cook until heated through. Add water 1 tablespoon at a time if the pan seems dry. Season with salt.

To assemble, in a large bowl, toss together the romaine, quinoa, black beans, corn, cherry tomatoes, and enough dressing to coat. Portion into bowls and top each serving with mashed avocado, smoky seitan, and Crispy Tortilla Strips, if desired. Dollop with Lime Sour Cream and serve with a lime wedge.

RAINBOW QUINOA SALAD

SERVES 4

3 tablespoons **seasoned rice vinegar**

2 tablespoons **toasted sesame oil**

2 tablespoons **agave nectar**

1 tablespoon **tamari**

3 cups cooked **quinoa**

1 small **carrot**, shredded or finely chopped

½ cup **cherry tomatoes**, halved

1 cup shelled **edamame**

¾ cup finely chopped **red cabbage**

3 **scallions**, thinly sliced

¼ cup **dried cranberries** or **cherries**

¼ cup coarsely chopped **almonds**

Sea salt

Sesame seeds, for garnish

I love the flavor of this protein-packed quinoa salad because it's very fresh and subtly sweet. When I feel like I've overeaten or just want something a little bit cleaner, I turn to this salad for lunch because it is packed with veggies and nutrients.

MAKE IT GLUTEN-FREE: Use gluten-free tamari.

In a small bowl, whisk together the vinegar, sesame oil, agave, and tamari. Set aside.

In a large bowl, toss together the quinoa, carrot, tomatoes, edamame, cabbage, scallions, cranberries, and almonds. Add the desired amount of dressing and toss to coat. Add salt to taste. Garnish with sesame seeds.

PEANUT KALE CRUNCH SALAD

SERVES 4

peanut dressing

½ cup **peanut butter**

¼ cup **seasoned rice vinegar**

¼ cup **water**

3 tablespoons **pure maple syrup**

1 tablespoon **sriracha**

1 teaspoon minced **fresh ginger**

1 small **garlic clove**, minced

½ teaspoon **sea salt**

marinated tempeh

¼ cup **water**

2 tablespoons **tamari**

2 tablespoons **pure maple syrup**

1 tablespoon **sriracha**

2 tablespoons **vegetable oil**

1 (8-ounce) package **tempeh**, cut into ¼-inch cubes

1 bunch **kale**, de-stemmed, leaves chopped very finely (about 4 cups)

2 cups cooked **quinoa** or **brown rice**

Toppings: Thinly sliced **scallions**; chopped roasted **peanuts**; **lime** wedges

This might just be my favorite salad ever because it's super sweet, spicy, and saucy—a flavor trifecta! If you're looking for a salad with a light vinaigrette, don't look for it here! This peanut dressing is so rich, delicious, and creamy that it could be used on more than just salad—try it on veggies, grains, noodles, etc. The tempeh is sweet and spicy, making it the perfect topper for this crave-worthy kale salad.

MAKE-AHEAD TIP: The peanut dressing can be made in advance and stored in an airtight container in the refrigerator for up to 5 days.

MAKE IT GLUTEN-FREE: Use gluten-free tamari.

Make the peanut dressing: Combine all the dressing ingredients in a blender and blend until smooth.

Make the marinated tempeh: Whisk together the water, tamari, maple syrup, and sriracha in a small bowl. In a large nonstick skillet, heat the oil over medium-high heat. When it shimmers, add the tempeh and cook, stirring, for about 5 minutes, until golden and lightly browned, adding more oil as needed. Add the liquid and stir to coat. Reduce the heat to medium-low and simmer for 5 to 10 minutes, until the sauce is thick.

To assemble, in a large bowl, toss together the kale and quinoa with enough dressing to coat. Portion into bowls and top each serving with the tempeh. Garnish with scallions and chopped peanuts, and serve with a lime wedge.

TRISHA YEARWOOD'S TOMATO BISQUE

SERVES 6

¾ cup **raw cashews** (see Tip, page 11)

¾ cup **water**

¼ cup **vegan margarine**

1 **onion**, diced

1 cup diced **carrots**

1 cup diced **celery**

3 **garlic cloves**, smashed

4 cups gluten-free **vegetable broth**

1 (28-ounce) can whole **fire-roasted tomatoes**, with their juices

1 tablespoon minced **fresh flat-leaf parsley**

1 teaspoon picked **fresh thyme leaves**

1 **bay leaf**

1½ teaspoons **sea salt**

Freshly ground **black pepper**

When Trisha Yearwood invited me to her home in Nashville to film a vegan episode of her Food Network cooking show, *Trisha's Southern Kitchen*, I almost died! Cooking with Trisha was a dream, not only because her vegan recipes rocked, but also because she is the sweetest, smartest, friendliest power-woman alive. Her tomato bisque was inspired by vegan chef Tal Ronnen, and it is pure genius. If it ain't broke, don't fix it!

In a blender, combine the cashews and water. Blend on high speed for about 2 minutes, until very smooth.

In a large saucepan, melt the margarine over medium heat. Add the onion, carrots, celery, and garlic and cook, stirring frequently, for about 10 minutes, until soft.

Add the broth, tomatoes and their juices, parsley, thyme, and bay leaf. Stir in the salt and season with pepper to taste. Increase the heat to high and bring to a boil, then reduce the heat to medium-low and simmer for about 30 minutes, until the flavors come together. Remove and discard the bay leaf, then stir in the cashew cream.

Working in batches, transfer the soup to a blender or food processor and blend on high speed until very smooth (be careful when blending hot liquids). Taste and adjust the seasoning. Ladle into bowls and serve.

TORTILLA SOUP

SERVES 4

2 tablespoons **vegetable oil**

1 **onion**, roughly chopped

3 small soft **corn tortillas**, torn into large strips

1½ teaspoons **sea salt**

¼ cup **tomato paste**

3 **garlic cloves**, minced

1 **jalapeño**, seeded and minced

1 tablespoon **taco seasoning**

¾ cup (6 ounces) **frozen sweet yellow corn**

3 cups **vegetable broth**

1 (14.5-ounce) can **fire-roasted diced tomatoes**, with their juices

⅛ teaspoon **cayenne pepper**

Freshly ground **black pepper**

toppings

Crispy Tortilla Strips (recipe follows)

Lime wedges

Chopped **fresh cilantro**

Diced **avocado** (optional)

Corn kernels (optional)

I love tortilla soup. I order it every time I see it on a menu (well, if it's vegan, of course). I created this recipe a few winters ago when my mom and I decided to do a Mexican theme for Christmas. We made guacamole and enchiladas and tacos galore, but the standout from the evening was surprisingly this Tortilla Soup. The lime wedge at the end is mandatory—it adds a touch of tang that you cannot do without.

MAKE IT GLUTEN-FREE: Make sure the corn tortillas in the soup and in the crispy tortilla strips are gluten-free.

In a large saucepan, heat the oil over medium-high heat. When it shimmers, add the onion and cook, stirring occasionally, for 5 to 7 minutes, until soft. Add the soft tortilla strips and season with the salt. Cook for about 1 minute. Add the tomato paste, garlic, jalapeño, and taco seasoning and cook for about 3 minutes, until fragrant. Add the corn, broth, and diced tomatoes and their juices and bring to a boil. Boil for about 5 minutes, until the flavors come together, then remove the pot from the heat.

Puree the soup directly in the pot using an immersion blender, or, working in batches, transfer the soup to a blender and puree until smooth (be careful when blending hot liquids); return the soup to the pot. Stir in the cayenne and black pepper to taste. Distribute the soup among bowls, then garnish with Crispy Tortilla Strips, lime wedges, cilantro, and other toppings as desired.

crispy tortilla strips

SERVES 4 TO 6

2 small soft **corn tortillas**   **Vegetable oil**, for frying

Using a pizza cutter or sharp knife, cut each tortilla into thin strips (about $\frac{1}{8}$ inch thick).

In a small skillet, heat $\frac{1}{2}$ inch of oil over medium-high heat until a small piece of tortilla sizzles when dropped into the oil. Gently place the tortilla strips into the heated oil, working in batches as necessary to avoid crowding the pan, and fry for about 2 minutes, until crisp, watching very carefully so that they don't burn. Remove with a slotted spoon and drain on paper towels.

SWEET CORN CHOWDER

SERVES 6

3 tablespoons **olive oil**

1 **onion**, coarsely chopped

1 **Yukon Gold** or other **yellow potato**, peeled and roughly chopped

6 cups (about 2 pounds) **frozen sweet yellow corn**

2 **garlic cloves**

1½ teaspoons **sea salt**

3 cups **vegetable broth**

¼ cup packed **light brown sugar**

¼ teaspoon **cayenne pepper**

1 **red bell pepper**, seeded and finely chopped

1 **jalapeño**, seeded and minced

Chloe's Croutons (page 85; optional)

Lime wedges, optional

Even in New York's summer heat, I still crave this hot-hot soup. Not only is it temperature hot, but it's also got a nice kick from the jalapeño. There is something very hydrating about the pureed corn, make it a great summer choice. It's flavorful and fun, with tons of color and texture.

MAKE IT GLUTEN-FREE: Use gluten-free broth and if serving with croutons, make them gluten-free.

In a large saucepan, heat 2 tablespoons of the olive oil over medium-high heat. When it shimmers, add the onion, potato, 4 cups of the corn, the garlic, and the salt. Cook, stirring occasionally, for 8 to 10 minutes, until the onion is translucent. Add the broth, brown sugar, and cayenne. Bring to a boil, then reduce the heat to medium and simmer for 15 minutes, until the potatoes are cooked through.

Turn off the heat and puree directly in the pot using an immersion blender, or, working in batches, carefully transfer the soup to a blender and puree until smooth (be careful when blending hot liquids); return the soup to the pot.

Meanwhile, in a large skillet, heat the remaining tablespoon of olive oil over medium heat. When it shimmers, add the bell pepper and remaining 2 cups of corn. Cook, stirring occasionally, for 5 to 7 minutes, until lightly browned, then add to the soup. Add the jalapeños and stir over medium heat until heated through. Taste and adjust the seasoning. Serve topped with croutons and a lime wedge, if desired.

hold on

SANDWICHES, BURGERS & TACOS

BACON LOVER'S BLT

SERVES 5

bacon

⅓ cup **coconut** or **vegetable oil**

⅓ cup **agave nectar**

¼ cup **tamari**

1 teaspoon **smoked paprika**

1 teaspoon **dried basil**

½ teaspoon **dried thyme**

½ teaspoon **ground cumin**

½ teaspoon **cayenne pepper**

½ teaspoon **garlic powder**

½ teaspoon **onion powder**

½ teaspoon **sea salt**

1 (8-ounce) package **tempeh**, sliced about ¼ inch thick

aioli

½ cup **vegan mayonnaise** or **silken tofu**

8 roasted **garlic cloves** (see Tip, opposite; optional)

1 tablespoon **lemon juice**

¼ teaspoon **sea salt**

2 **avocados**

2 teaspoons **lemon juice**

Sea salt

10 slices **whole-grain bread**, toasted

Toppings: **Green-leaf** or **romaine lettuce**; sliced **tomato**; sliced **red onion**

This sandwich alone can turn a bacon-loving carnivore into a piglet-hugging vegan. The "bacon" is made from tempeh, a fermented soybean product, which has a hearty, nutty texture and soaks up all the delicious flavor of the marinade.

NOTE: The bacon will be best if it marinates for a few hours or overnight before being cooked.

MAKE IT GLUTEN-FREE: Use gluten-free tamari and serve on gluten-free bread.

Make the bacon: In a medium bowl, combine the coconut oil, agave, tamari, spices, and salt. Add the tempeh and toss to coat. Transfer to a zip-top plastic bag and marinate in the refrigerator for at least 3 hours or up to overnight.

Heat a large nonstick skillet over medium-high heat. Remove the tempeh from the marinade, allowing any excess to drip off; reserve the marinade. When the skillet is hot, toss in the tempeh. Panfry for 6 to 8 minutes, until lightly browned on both sides. Add a little of the reserved marinade to the pan for extra flavor.

Make the aioli: In a blender or food processor, combine all the aioli ingredients and blend until smooth.

Combine the avocado, lemon juice, and salt in a medium bowl. Mash with the back of a fork until the avocado is broken down but still chunky. Season with salt.

To assemble, spread once slice of bread with aioli, then layer with some bacon, avocado, lettuce, tomato, and onion. Place a second slice of bread on top and secure with a toothpick. Repeat with the remaining ingredients.

 ROASTING GARLIC

Preheat the oven to 375°F.

Peel away the papery outer layers of the garlic bulb, but leave the individual garlic skins intact. Slice off the pointy end of the head of garlic, so that the tips of all cloves are exposed. Place the head of garlic in aluminum foil, cut-side up, and drizzle with oil and season with salt and pepper. Loosely fold up the ends of the foil pouch and pinch to seal. Roast for 30 to 40 minutes, until the garlic cloves are fork tender. Remove from the oven and let cool. Once cooled, squeeze the head of garlic and the soft cloves will pop out.

PESTO BEET BURGERS

SERVES 4 TO 6

patties

1 tablespoon **olive oil**, plus more as needed

1 **onion**, finely chopped

2 **garlic cloves**, minced

3 medium **beets** (about 5 ounces each), peeled and grated

1 cup cooked **brown rice**

½ cup **bread crumbs**

1 teaspoon **sea salt**

1 teaspoon freshly ground **black pepper**

pesto

½ cup **raw cashews** (see Tip, page 11)

2 **garlic cloves**

1½ tablespoons **lemon juice**

1 teaspoon **sea salt**

¼ cup **vegetable** or **olive oil**

¼ cup **water**

2 ounces fresh **basil**

Freshly ground **black pepper**

to assemble

8 **whole-grain buns**, toasted

Arugula

Pickled Red Onion (page 115)

Beet burgers are all the rage these days because the pink, beety juices tint the patty to a hue that resembles rare meat. I know, some of you might find that comparison far from appealing, but if it ropes in carnivores for a vegan lunch, I'm all for it! Pink and green is one of my favorite color combos, so I like slathering this burger with a bright green pesto sauce.

MAKE-AHEAD TIP: The patties can be made in advance and stored in an airtight container in the refrigerator for up to 5 days or in the freezer for up to 1 month. Cook directly from refrigerated or frozen.

MAKE IT GLUTEN-FREE: Use gluten-free bread crumbs and serve on gluten-free buns.

In a large nonstick skillet, heat the olive oil over medium-high heat. When it shimmers, add the onion and cook, stirring occasionally, for about 5 minutes, until soft and lightly browned. Add the garlic and beets, and cook for about 5 minutes more to soften the raw beets, stirring often. Transfer to a food processor; set the skillet aside (no need to wash it).

Add the brown rice, bread crumbs, salt, and pepper to the food processor. Pulse until the ingredients just come together, about 20 pulses. Adjust the seasoning to taste. Form the mixture into patties with the palms of your hands.

Lightly grease the same skillet you used for the onion, and heat over medium-high heat. When it shimmers, working in batches, add the patties and cook for about 4 minutes on each side, until they are nicely browned. Add more oil to the pan as needed between batches.

— hold on —

Make the pesto: In a blender, combine the cashews, garlic, lemon juice, salt, oil, and water and blend for about 2 minutes, until very smooth. Add the basil and blend again until well combined.

To assemble, on each bun, layer the pesto, a burger patty, arugula, pickled onions, and more pesto.

BRUSSELS SPROUTS TACOS

SERVES 4

brussels sprouts

1 tablespoon **vegetable oil**

8 ounces shredded **Brussels sprouts** (about 2 cups)

1 tablespoon **taco seasoning**

¼ teaspoon **sea salt**

corn

1 tablespoon **vegetable oil**

2 cups **frozen sweet yellow corn**

¼ teaspoon **sea salt**

½ **jalapeño**, seeded and minced

2 teaspoons **lime juice**

1 teaspoon **agave nectar**

When most people think of tacos, they think of carnitas or carne asada. But I swear to the vegan gods, these Brussels sprouts are so savory you'll forget that they're missing the meat. I made them with my friends Ann Marie and Susan, thinking we were just throwing together a quick, basic lunch, but it turns out these were drop-dead delicious! Ann Marie took home the recipe and tried it on her son—if a six-year-old gives two thumbs up to Brussels sprouts, you know you've worked a little magic.

MAKE IT GLUTEN-FREE: Make sure the corn tortillas are gluten-free.

Make the Brussels sprouts: In a large skillet, heat the oil over medium-high heat. When it shimmers, add the Brussels sprouts, taco seasoning, and salt. Cook, stirring continuously, for about 10 minutes, until the Brussels are slightly softened and charred.

Meanwhile, make the corn: In a separate large skillet, heat the oil over medium-high heat. When it shimmers, add the corn and salt and cook, stirring frequently, for 5 to 7 minutes, until charred. Remove the skillet from the heat and mix in the jalapeño, lime juice, and agave. Taste and adjust the seasoning.

hold on

chimichurri sauce

¼ cup **raw cashews** (see Tip, page 11)

¼ cup **water**

½ cup chopped **fresh cilantro**

½ cup chopped **fresh flat-leaf parsley**

¼ cup **canola oil**

3 tablespoons **lemon juice**

2 **garlic cloves**

2 tablespoons **agave nectar**

¼ teaspoon **ground cumin**

1 teaspoon **sea salt**

½ teaspoon freshly ground **black pepper**

to assemble

8 to 12 small soft **corn tortillas**

Chopped **fresh cilantro**

Lime wedges

Pickled Red Onion (recipe follows; optional)

Make the chimichurri sauce: In a blender or food processor, blend all the chimichurri ingredients until smooth.

To assemble, heat a tortilla in a pan over medium-high heat or by placing it directly on the burner over medium-low heat for about 20 to 30 seconds on each side, using tongs to flip. Layer on some of the corn, Brussels sprouts, and a drizzle of chimichurri sauce. Repeat with the remaining tortillas and filling. Garnish each with cilantro, a lime wedge, and Pickled Red Onion, if desired.

pickled red onion

MAKES ABOUT ½ CUP

½ **red onion**, thinly sliced

⅔ cup **seasoned rice vinegar**

Put the red onion in a small bowl and cover with the vinegar. Toss to combine and let sit for 1 to 2 hours, until the onions soften. Store in an airtight container in the refrigerator for up to 2 weeks.

CAULIFLOWER
AL PASTOR TACOS

SERVES 4

About 3 cups (12 ounces) **cauliflower florets**, cut into bite-size pieces

1 (8-ounce) can **pineapple** chunks, drained and cut into bite-size pieces

2 tablespoons **olive oil**

2 teaspoons **taco seasoning**

½ teaspoon **sea salt**

8 small soft **corn tortillas**

Cashew Queso (recipe follows)

toppings

Pickled Red Onions (page 115)

Sliced **avocado** or **guacamole**

Chopped **fresh cilantro**

Lime wedges

Tacos *al pastor* traditionally refers to pork marinated in spices and pineapple. This vegan version switches up the pork for cauliflower while capturing the spicy seasonings and juicy pineapple. I served these to my taco-loving boyfriend, Ben, and he said they were the best he's ever had! Now, whether they were *really* the best tacos he's ever had or it was just the Cashew Queso talking is a mystery still unsolved . . .

MAKE IT GLUTEN-FREE: Make sure the corn tortillas are gluten-free.

Preheat the oven to 425°F.

Put the cauliflower and pineapple on a rimmed baking sheet and toss with the olive oil, taco seasoning, and salt. Arrange in an even layer and roast for 20 to 30 minutes, until the cauliflower is fork-tender and nicely charred. Taste and adjust the seasoning.

Heat a tortilla in a pan over medium-high heat or by placing it directly on the burner over medium-low heat for 20 to 30 seconds on each side, until lightly browned. Use tongs to flip. Layer on some of the cauliflower, Cashew Queso, pickled onions, and avocado. Garnish with cilantro and serve with lime wedges.

— hold on —

cashew queso

MAKES 2½ CUPS

 1 cup **water**

1 cup **raw cashews** (see Tip, page 11)

2 tablespoons **nutritional yeast flakes**

4 ounces canned **tomato sauce** (about ⅓ cup)

1 teaspoon **sea salt**

½ teaspoon **chili powder**

¼ teaspoon **ground turmeric**

¼ teaspoon **cayenne pepper**

2 teaspoons **agave nectar**

In a blender, combine all the ingredients and blend until smooth. Transfer to a small saucepan and stir over medium-low heat for about 5 minutes, until warmed through and thickened.

COCONUT FALAFEL SLIDERS WITH MANGO SALSA
MAKES 8 SLIDERS

falafel

1 (15.5-ounce) can **chickpeas**, drained, rinsed, and patted dry

½ **red onion**, finely diced

¼ cup all-purpose **flour**, plus more if needed

¼ cup coarsely chopped **fresh flat-leaf parsley** or **cilantro**

3 **garlic cloves**, minced

½ teaspoon **ground cumin**

½ teaspoon **sea salt**

5 grinds freshly ground **black pepper**

1 cup **shredded coconut**

Vegetable or **coconut oil**, for frying

apricot-mustard sauce

¾ cup **apricot jam**

1½ tablespoons **Dijon mustard**

8 **mini buns** or **dinner rolls**, halved and toasted

optional toppings

Lettuce

Thinly sliced **tomato**

Thinly sliced **red onion**

Mango-Jalapeño Salsa (page 122)

Lime wedges

Everybody loves coconut, but vegans especially love coconut. We put it in our curries, smoothies, soups, and desserts. We love coconut milk because it's nature's substitute for heavy cream, and we love coconut meat and flakes because the texture can elevate our dishes. I've always had a case of FOMO (that's "fear of missing out") when it comes to coconut shrimp because the concept of sweet, crispy, coconutty flakes coating a savory food is brilliant. So here I hold the shrimp, but use the crust on falafel sliders instead.

NOTE: For a shortcut, just make the falafel and buy pre-made mango salsa.

MAKE-AHEAD TIP: The falafel can be made in advance and stored in an airtight container in the refrigerator for up to 5 days or in the freezer for up to 1 month. Cook directly from refrigerated or frozen.

MAKE IT GLUTEN-FREE: Use gluten-free coconut, mustard, and flour (or chickpea flour) and serve on gluten-free buns.

Make the falafel: Combine the chickpeas, onion, flour, parsley, garlic, cumin, salt, and pepper in a food processor. Pulse just a few times until the mixture almost comes together; do not overprocess. If the mixture is too sticky, add a little more flour. Using your hands, form the mixture into mini patties, about 2 inches in diameter and ½ inch thick.

Place the shredded coconut on a plate. Dredge each patty in the shredded coconut, pressing to adhere.

In a large skillet, heat the oil over medium-high heat. When it shimmers, add the patties, working in batches as needed, and cook for 3 to 5 minutes on each side, or until nicely browned. Add more oil between batches as needed.

Make the sauce: In a small saucepan, combine the jam and mustard and cook over medium heat, stirring frequently, for about 3 minutes, until warmed through.

On each bun, layer lettuce, tomato, onion, falafel, sauce, and/or Mango-Jalapeño Salsa. Serve warm, with a lime wedge on the side.

MANGO-GUACAMOLE CRUNCH BURGERS

SERVES 6 TO 8

black bean patties

2 tablespoons **olive oil**, plus more as needed

1 **onion**, finely chopped

1 (15-ounce) can **black beans**, drained and rinsed

1 cup mashed cooked **sweet potato** (1 medium sweet potato)

½ cup **bread crumbs**

3 tablespoons **sriracha**

2 teaspoons **sea salt**

½ cup cooked **brown rice**

smashed avocado

2 **avocados**

1 tablespoon **lime juice**

Sea salt

mango-jalapeño salsa

1 **mango**, finely diced

1 **jalapeño**, seeded and minced

1 tablespoon **lime juice**

2 teaspoons **agave nectar**

to assemble

Burger buns, toasted

Lettuce

Sliced **tomato**

Sliced **red onion**

Crispy Tortilla Strips (page 101; optional)

As a born-and-bred avoholic, I knew I needed to make a veggie burger that was centered around avocado. The earliest versions were too mushy. (Maybe a whole avocado per burger was a *little* overboard . . .) Then I added crispy tortilla strips and lettuce, tomato, and onion; all this added texture completed (or should I say, crunchified) the experience.

NOTE: For a shortcut, use store-bought guacamole. Also, you can freeze extra uncooked patties for later use (simply panfry straight from frozen when you want to eat them).

MAKE IT GLUTEN-FREE: Use gluten-free bread crumbs and tortilla strips and serve on gluten-free buns.

Make the black bean patties: In a large nonstick skillet, heat 1 tablespoon of the olive oil over medium heat. When it shimmers, add the onion and cook for about 20 minutes, until tender and slightly caramelized. Transfer the onion to a large bowl; set the skillet aside (no need to wash it).

Add the beans, sweet potato, bread crumbs, sriracha, salt, and brown rice to the bowl with the onion. Using a large spoon or your hands, mix to combine. Using your hands, form the bean mixture into patties to match the size of your buns.

In the same skillet in which you cooked the onion, heat the remaining tablespoon of oil over medium-high heat. When it shimmers, working in batches, add the patties and cook for about 3 minutes on each side, until lightly browned and crisp. Add more oil between batches as needed. Transfer the patties to paper towels to drain.

Make the smashed avocado: In a medium bowl, lightly mash the avocado and the lime juice. Season with salt.

Make the mango-jalapeño salsa: In a small bowl, toss all the salsa ingredients together.

— hold on —

To assemble, on each bottom bun, layer a black bean patty, lettuce, tomato, onion, smashed avocado, mango salsa, and/or Crispy Tortilla Strips. Top with the bun tops and enjoy.

HAWAIIAN TERIYAKI SLIDERS

MAKES 10 SLIDERS

1 (20-ounce) can **pineapple slices** in juice

2 tablespoons **olive oil**, plus more as needed

About 2½ cups (8 ounces) sliced **mushrooms**

1 (15-ounce) can **lentils**, drained and rinsed, or 1½ cups cooked lentils

½ cup all-purpose **flour**, plus more if needed

1 teaspoon **sea salt**

1 teaspoon freshly ground **black pepper**

¼ teaspoon **crushed red pepper flakes**

¼ cup **teriyaki sauce**

10 **Mini buns** or **dinner rolls**, sliced in half and toasted

Toppings: Thinly sliced **scallions**; white or black **sesame seeds**

These sliders are super easy to make and even easier to pop in your mouth. When my friend Nancy asked for recipe ideas for a Super Bowl party, I suggested this. She ended up making them and the verdict was: Touchdown! (That means they were good, right?) All her neighbors gobbled them up so fast, they didn't even realize they were vegan.

MAKE IT GLUTEN-FREE: Use gluten-free baking flour, make sure the teriyaki sauce is gluten-free, and serve on gluten-free buns.

Heat a large nonstick skillet over medium-high heat. Lay the pineapple slices in the pan, reserving the juice in the can and working in batches as needed to avoid overcrowding. Cook for 3 to 4 minutes on each side, until lightly browned. Then pour in the juice, reduce the heat to medium, and let it bubble and caramelize, about 3 minutes. Transfer to a plate.

In the same skillet, heat 1 tablespoon of the olive oil over medium-high heat. When it shimmers, add the mushrooms and cook, stirring occasionally, for 3 to 5 minutes, until softened. Transfer the mushrooms to a food processor; set the skillet aside (no need to wash it). Add the lentils, flour, salt, black pepper, and red pepper flakes to the food processor and pulse just a few times until the mixture almost comes together; do not overprocess. If the mixture is too sticky, add a little more flour. Using the palms of your hands, form the mixture into mini patties, each about 2 inches in diameter and ½ inch thick.

In the same skillet, heat the remaining tablespoon of olive oil over medium-high heat. Working in batches, add the patties and cook for 3 to 4 minutes on each side, until nicely browned, adding more oil between batches as needed. Add the teriyaki sauce to the skillet and cook until the sauce thickens and coats the patties.

On each bun, layer a slider, additional teriyaki sauce, caramelized pineapple, scallions, and sesame seeds. Serve warm.

MEATBALL PARM

SERVES 4

mozzarella sauce

¾ cup **raw cashews** (see Tip, page 11)

½ cup **water**

½ teaspoon **sea salt**

½ teaspoon **garlic powder**

Juice of ½ **lemon**

meatballs

About 2 medium (3 ounces) **roasted beets** (see Tip, page 12)

1 cup cooked **brown rice**

8 ounces **seitan** (strips or cubed), drained well

¼ cup **bread crumbs**

1 **garlic clove**, minced

1 teaspoon **sea salt**

¼ teaspoon freshly ground **black pepper**

¼ teaspoon **dried oregano**

¼ teaspoon **crushed red pepper flakes**

1 tablespoon **olive oil**, plus more as needed

to assemble

4 **hot dog buns**, toasted

2 cups store-bought **marinara sauce**, heated

Vegan Parmesan (page 55)

Chopped **fresh basil**

This recipe has a handful of components to it (maybe not the best choice for a busy weeknight!), but if you put in the time, I promise the result will be showstopping, both to the eyes and the taste buds! I recommend making the meatballs and mozzarella sauce the day before serving to break up the prep.

MAKE-AHEAD TIP: The mozzarella sauce can be made in advance and stored in an airtight container in the refrigerator for up to 3 days. The meatballs can be made in advance, formed into balls, and stored in an airtight container in the refrigerator for up to 5 days or in the freezer for up to 1 month. Cook directly from refrigerated or frozen.

Make the mozzarella sauce: In a blender, combine all the sauce ingredients. Blend on high speed for about 2 minutes, until very smooth.

Make the meatballs: In a food processor, combine the beets, brown rice, seitan, bread crumbs, garlic, salt, black pepper, oregano, and red pepper flakes. Process until well-combined. Using your hands, form the mixture into 1- to 2-inch balls (they should be able to fit into the buns).

In a large nonstick skillet, heat the olive oil over medium-high heat. When it shimmers, add the meatballs and cook, turning occasionally, for 8 to 10 minutes, until browned all over, adding more oil as needed. Transfer to paper towels to drain.

To assemble, on each bun, layer a spoonful of marinara sauce, meatballs, and a drizzle of mozzarella sauce. Garnish with Vegan Parmesan and basil, and serve warm.

SLOPPY CHLO'S

SERVES 6

2 tablespoons **olive oil**

1 **onion**, finely chopped

1 **green bell pepper**, finely chopped

2½ cups (8 ounces) **mushrooms**, finely chopped

4 **garlic cloves**, minced

1½ teaspoons **sea salt**

1 teaspoon **chili powder**

¼ teaspoon **crushed red pepper flakes**

1 (15-ounce) can **lentils**, drained and rinsed, or 1½ cups cooked lentils

1 (15-ounce) can **tomato sauce**

2 tablespoons **light brown sugar**

Freshly ground **black pepper**

6 **hamburger buns**, toasted

My vegan version of sloppy joes are every bit as fun and saucy, but way healthier than their beefy counterpart. Instead of meat, I use lentils and mushrooms simmered in tangy, tomato-y goodness. Guilt-free and loaded with flavor.

MAKE IT GLUTEN-FREE: Serve on gluten-free buns.

In a large saucepan, heat the olive oil over medium-high heat. When it shimmers, add the onion and bell pepper and cook, stirring occasionally, for 5 to 7 minutes, until softened. Add the mushrooms and cook, stirring frequently, for 8 to 10 minutes, until almost soft. Add the garlic, salt, chili powder, and red pepper flakes and cook for about 1 minute more, until fragrant.

Stir in the lentils, tomato sauce, and brown sugar, scraping up any browned bits from the bottom of the pan. Season with black pepper and reduce the heat to medium. Simmer, uncovered, stirring occasionally, for about 10 minutes, until the flavors come together. Taste and adjust the seasoning.

Spoon onto buns and serve.

TANGY MAPLE
BBQ BURGERS

SERVES 4

bbq sauce

1 (8-ounce) can **tomato sauce**

3 tablespoons **pure maple syrup**

3 tablespoons **lime juice**

2 tablespoons **tamari**

1 **garlic clove**

½ teaspoon **ground cumin**

¼ teaspoon **cayenne pepper**

1 (8-ounce) can **pineapple slices** in juice

2 tablespoons **olive oil**

8 ounces **seitan strips**

About 1 cup (5 ounces) **shiitake** or **oyster mushrooms**, de-stemmed and thinly sliced

4 cups (1 bunch) chopped **greens** (kale, collards, or chard)

Sea salt

4 **hamburger buns** or **ciabatta rolls**, toasted

This vegan burger is super popular among BBQ lovers because isn't it really about the sauce at the end of the day?! Caramelizing the pineapple in its own juice is a technique my friend Dustin, @TheVeganRoadie, taught me—and I think that's what gives these burgers that special something.

Make the BBQ sauce: Combine all the BBQ sauce ingredients in a blender or food processor and blend until smooth.

To caramelize the pineapple, heat a nonstick skillet over medium-high heat. Place the pineapple slices in the pan, reserving the juice, working in batches as needed. Cook until lightly browned on both sides. Add the juice, reduce the heat to medium, and let the juice bubble down and caramelize, about 3 minutes. Set aside.

In a large nonstick skillet, heat the olive oil over medium heat. When it shimmers, add the seitan and mushrooms and cook for about 10 minutes, until nicely browned. Add the greens and cook, stirring occasionally, until softened. Season with salt. Add the BBQ sauce to the skillet and cook, stirring occasionally, for about 3 minutes, until the sauce thickens and the seitan is nicely coated. If you prefer a sweeter BBQ sauce, add more maple syrup to taste.

Layer some of the BBQ seitan, greens, and caramelized pineapple on each bun. Serve warm.

hold on

oh, the
pastabilities!

NOODLES & PASTA

5-INGREDIENT KALE PESTO PASTA

SERVES 4 TO 6

1 pound **linguine**

4 cups (about 1 bunch) chopped **curly kale leaves**

½ cup **raw cashews** (see Tip, page 11)

½ cup **olive oil**

3 **garlic cloves**, minced

2 tablespoons **lemon juice**

1 teaspoon **sea salt**

Freshly ground **black pepper**

Crushed red pepper flakes (optional)

Not including the kitchen staples of olive oil, salt, and pepper, this pesto is only five ingredients, but it rates 100 on the flavor scale! If you love simplicity, this dish is for you. If not, well, add some sun-dried tomatoes for an extra tangy punch.

MAKE IT GLUTEN-FREE: Use gluten-free pasta.

Bring a large pot of heavily salted water to a boil over high heat. Add the pasta and cook to al dente according to the package directions. Drain the pasta and return it to the pot, off the heat.

Meanwhile, in a food processor, combine the kale, cashews, olive oil, garlic, lemon juice, and salt and process until smooth. Season with black pepper.

Toss the pesto with the pasta. Portion onto plates and top each serving with a pinch of red pepper flakes, if desired.

BEET FETTUCCINE ALFREDO WITH BASIL RICOTTA

SERVES 4 TO 6

1 pound **fettuccine**

1 tablespoon **olive oil**

1 **onion**, chopped

3 **garlic cloves**, minced

1 (16-ounce) package **silken tofu**

About 2 medium (3 ounces) **roasted beets** (see Tip, page 12)

½ cup **water**, plus more as needed

2 tablespoons **lemon juice**

2½ teaspoons **sea salt**

toppings

Basil Ricotta (recipe follows)

Freshly ground **black pepper**

Vegan Parmesan (page 55)

Chopped **fresh basil**

The pretty pink color of this pasta is mesmerizing. It's almost too pretty to eat . . . almost. Pro tip: Don't throw out the beet greens! They are softer than kale but sturdier than spinach. I like to sauté them to add to my pasta for a more nutritious and complete meal.

MAKE-AHEAD TIP: The sauce can be made in advance and stored in an airtight container in the refrigerator for up to 3 days.

MAKE IT GLUTEN-FREE: Use gluten-free pasta.

Bring a large pot of heavily salted water to a boil over high heat. Add the pasta and cook to al dente according to the package directions. Drain the pasta and return it to the pot, off the heat.

Meanwhile, in a medium skillet, heat the olive oil over medium-high heat. When it shimmers, add the onion and cook for 5 to 7 minutes, until softened. Add the garlic and cook for about 1 minute more, until fragrant. Remove the skillet from the heat.

In a blender, combine the onion and garlic mixture, tofu, beets, water, lemon juice, and salt. Blend on high speed for about 2 minutes, until very smooth.

Toss the pasta with the desired amount of sauce. Taste and adjust the seasoning. If the sauce gets too thick, add more water, 1 tablespoon at a time. Portion onto plates and top with the Basil Ricotta, pepper, Vegan Parmesan, and basil.

basil ricotta

MAKES ABOUT 3 CUPS

1 tablespoon **olive oil**

1 large **onion**, coarsely chopped

3 **garlic cloves**

1 (16-ounce) package **extra-firm tofu**, drained

2 tablespoons **lemon juice**

2 teaspoons **sea salt**

1 teaspoon freshly ground **black pepper**

2 cups chopped **fresh basil**

In a large skillet, heat the olive oil over medium heat. When it shimmers, add the onion and cook, stirring occasionally, for 5 to 7 minutes, until softened. Transfer the onion to a food processor. Add the garlic, tofu, lemon juice, salt, and pepper. Process until smooth. Taste and adjust the seasoning. Pulse in the basil until well incorporated. Store in an airtight container in the refrigerator for up to 2 days.

CORN CARBONARA

SERVES 4 TO 6

1 pound **spaghetti**

4 cups (about 1 pound) **frozen sweet yellow corn**

2 tablespoons **olive oil**

1 large **onion**, chopped

4 **garlic cloves**, minced

2 tablespoons **pure maple syrup**

2 teaspoons **sea salt**

¼ teaspoon **cayenne pepper**

¼ cup **water**, plus more as needed

2 tablespoons **lemon juice**

Toppings: Freshly ground **black pepper**; chopped **fresh basil**; halved **cherry tomatoes**

Carbonara is traditionally made with egg, bacon, and a lot of cheese. So how do you make it vegan? Well, this recipe is kind of amazing. There is no dairy, no cashew cream, no tofu, no nothing! But somehow it gets *so* creamy. The trick is simply pureed corn for an ultra-saucy summer pasta carbonara.

MAKE IT GLUTEN-FREE: Use gluten-free pasta.

Bring a large pot of heavily salted water to a boil over medium-high heat. Add the pasta and cook to al dente according to the package directions. Just before draining it, add 1 cup of the corn to the pot and let thaw for about 30 seconds. Drain the pasta and corn and return both to the pot, off the heat.

Meanwhile, in a large skillet, heat the olive oil over medium-high heat. When it shimmers, add the onion and cook for 5 to 7 minutes, until softened. Add the garlic, the remaining 3 cups of corn, the maple syrup, salt, and cayenne and cook for about 3 minutes, until heated through. Transfer the mixture to a blender or food processor. Add the water and lemon juice and blend on high speed for about 2 minutes, until very smooth.

Add the sauce to the pot with the pasta and corn and toss to coat. If the sauce gets too thick, add water, 1 tablespoon at a time, until the desired consistency is reached. Taste and adjust the seasoning. Portion onto plates and top with black pepper, basil, and cherry tomatoes. Serve immediately.

CREAMY TOMATO-BASIL SPAGHETTINI

SERVES 4 TO 6

1 pound **spaghettini** or **thin spaghetti**

2 tablespoons **olive oil**

3 **garlic cloves**, minced

½ teaspoon **dried oregano**

1 (28-ounce) can **whole peeled tomatoes**, with their juices

2 teaspoons **sea salt**

2 tablespoons **light brown sugar**

½ cup **coconut cream** (see Note)

½ cup chopped **fresh basil**, plus more for garnish

Freshly ground **black pepper**

Somehow this pasta feels so light, yet so rich and creamy at the same time. Finishing it off with a touch of coconut cream gives a fullness to the flavor and texture. I can still eat bowls and bowls and bowls of it and never hit a pasta coma. This is my go-to dish after a stressful day when I need comfort and deliciousness.

NOTE: In order to get coconut "cream," stick a can of coconut milk in the refrigerator overnight. The liquid and fat will naturally separate, and the cream will rise to the top! Scoop out what you need and save the rest for later use.

MAKE-AHEAD TIP: The sauce can be made in advance and stored in an airtight container in the refrigerator for up to 3 days.

MAKE IT GLUTEN-FREE: Use gluten-free pasta.

Bring a large pot of heavily salted water to a boil over high heat. Add the pasta and cook to al dente according to the package directions. Drain the pasta and return it to the pot, off the heat.

Meanwhile, in a large, deep skillet, heat the olive oil over medium heat. When it shimmers, add the garlic and oregano and cook for about 1 minute, until fragrant. Stir in the tomatoes and their juices, the salt, and brown sugar. Bring to a simmer, stirring occasionally, and cook for about 5 minutes, until the flavors come together.

Transfer the tomato mixture to a blender or food processor and add the coconut cream. Blend until smooth. Add the sauce to the pot with the pasta. Add the basil and toss to combine. If the sauce gets too thick, add water, 1 tablespoon at a time, until the desired consistency is reached. Taste and adjust the seasoning. Portion onto plates and top with pepper and basil.

SOY-GINGER SOBA NOODLES

SERVES 4 TO 6

8 to 10 ounces **soba noodles**

1 cup shelled **edamame**

¼ cup **seasoned rice vinegar**

¼ cup **toasted sesame oil**

2 tablespoons **tamari**

2 tablespoons **pure maple syrup**

2 teaspoons minced **fresh ginger**

Half a **garlic clove**

3 **scallions**, thinly sliced

2 tablespoons **white** or **black sesame seeds**

Sea salt

Optional toppings: **Cucumber**, **radish**, or **carrot**, cut into matchsticks (see Tip, below)

Soba noodles are made from buckwheat, which is high in fiber and protein, making it a superstar pasta choice. This flavorful dish is great for a light meal or a filling side dish, plus you can get creative with what you add on top. Try veggies, Marinated Tempeh (page 96), or whatever else you like!

MAKE IT GLUTEN-FREE: Use gluten-free soba noodles and gluten-free tamari.

Bring a large pot of heavily salted water to a boil over high heat. Add the noodles and cook according to the package directions. Add the edamame to the boiling noodles right before draining. Drain the noodles and edamame, and rinse with cold water. Transfer to a large bowl.

Meanwhile, in a blender or food processor, combine the vinegar, sesame oil, tamari, maple syrup, ginger, and garlic. Blend until combined, then add the sauce to the noodles. Add the scallions, and sesame seeds and toss to combine. Add salt to taste and garnish with veggie matchsticks, if desired. Serve chilled or at room temperature.

TIP MATCH(STICK) MAKING

Cutting veggies into matchsticks—formally known as julienne—is a technique I learned in my knife skills class in culinary school at the Natural Gourmet Institute. It's the perfect shape for slaws, salads, and pastas. To keep the radish from rolling around while you work, cut off a slim piece to make a flat edge to stabilize it. Then cut thin strips lengthwise and lay them next to each other. Cut ⅛-inch strips so that the resulting shape is approximately ⅛ inch x ⅛ inch x 2 inches.

EASY PAD THAI

SERVES 4 TO 6

8 ounces **rice noodles**

sauce

¼ cup **apricot** or **mango jam**

3 tablespoons **light brown sugar**

2 tablespoons **tamari**

2 tablespoons **seasoned rice vinegar**

1 tablespoon **tomato paste**

1 teaspoon **sea salt**

¼ teaspoon **ground turmeric**

2 tablespoons **vegetable oil**

1 **red bell pepper**, thinly sliced

½ cup **snow peas**

½ cup **sliced carrots** (I like carrot "chips" for this recipe)

2 **scallions**, thinly sliced

1 **garlic clove**, minced

Sea salt

1 **lime**, cut into wedges

½ cup **peanuts**, finely chopped

Chopped **fresh cilantro**, for garnish (optional)

Drizzle of **sriracha** (optional)

When it comes to takeout, pad thai is my weakness. But I love making it at home, too, because my version of the recipe actually tastes like takeout without the grease and risk of egg or fish sauce contamination! Oh, and I can add all the extra veggies I want—no extra charge!

MAKE IT GLUTEN-FREE: Use gluten-free tamari.

Bring a large pot of heavily salted water to a boil over high heat. Add the noodles and cook according to the package directions. Drain and rinse with cold water.

Make the sauce: In a small bowl, whisk together all the sauce ingredients.

In a large nonstick skillet, heat the oil over medium-high heat. When it shimmers, add the bell pepper, snow peas, carrots, scallions, and garlic. Season lightly with salt and cook for about 5 minutes, until the vegetables are slightly softened and lightly browned. Add the noodles and sauce and cook, tossing frequently, for 2 to 3 minutes, until the noodles and vegetables are coated and the sauce thickens. If the sauce gets too thick, add water, 1 tablespoon at a time, until the desired consistency is reached. Top each serving with a lime wedge, peanuts, and cilantro and/or sriracha, if desired.

MATCHA SOBA WITH SPICY TOFU NUGGETS

SERVES 4

8 to 10 ounces **soba noodles**

creamy matcha sauce

1 tablespoon **vegetable oil**

1 small **onion**, chopped

3 **garlic cloves**, minced

½ cup **raw cashews** (see Tip, page 11)

1 cup **water**

2 teaspoons **pure maple syrup**

1 teaspoon **lemon juice**

1½ teaspoons **sea salt**

1 teaspoon **matcha green tea powder**

tofu nuggets

2 tablespoons **vegetable oil**

1 (16-ounce) package **extra-firm tofu**, pressed (see Tip, page 14) and cut into ¼-inch cubes

2 tablespoons **tamari**

2 tablespoons **pure maple syrup**

1 tablespoon **sriracha**

Toppings: Thinly sliced **scallions**; **white** or **black sesame seeds**

I love creamy pastas like fettuccine Alfredo, but I also love the spices and flavors of Asian cuisine. I decided to meld my two loves into one creamy and comforting yet bold and spicy dish that revolves around my greatest love of all—matcha!

MAKE-AHEAD TIP: The creamy matcha sauce can be made in advance and stored in an airtight container in the refrigerator for up to 3 days.

MAKE IT GLUTEN-FREE: Use gluten-free soba noodles and gluten-free tamari.

Bring a large pot of heavily salted water to a boil over high heat. Add the noodles and cook according to the package directions. Drain and rinse with cold water. Return the noodles to the pot, off the heat.

Make the matcha sauce: In a large nonstick skillet, heat the oil over medium-high heat. When it shimmers, add the onion and cook for 5 to 7 minutes, until softened. Add the garlic and cook for about 1 minute more, until fragrant. Transfer the mixture to a blender, reserving skillet for later use. Add the cashews, water, maple syrup, lemon juice, salt, and matcha. Blend on high speed for about 2 minutes, until very smooth.

Meanwhile, make the tofu: In reserved skillet, heat the oil over medium-high heat. When it shimmers, add the tofu and cook for about 3 minutes on each side, until golden all over. Add the tamari, maple syrup, and sriracha, reduce the heat to medium, and cook for about 5 minutes, until the tofu is evenly coated and the sauce has thickened.

Over low heat, add the sauce to the pot of noodles and toss to coat, about 2 minutes, until heated through. Taste and adjust the seasoning. Top each serving with tofu nuggets, scallions, and sesame seeds.

WHITE SHELLS & CHEESE
SERVES 4 TO 6

About 3 cups (12 ounces) **cauliflower florets**

8 **garlic cloves**

¼ cup **olive oil**

2½ teaspoons **sea salt**

1 pound **medium pasta shells**

2½ cups **water**

½ cup **raw cashews** (see Tip, page 11)

1 tablespoon **lemon juice**

Freshly ground **black pepper**

Vegan Parmesan (page 55)

Some days you just need a hot bubble bath, other days a big glass of wine, and others still, what you really need is creamy cauliflower shells to remind you that everything is going to be okay. This dish is a big ol' bowl of comfort. Leave the recipe as is for kid-friendly food, or add a drizzle of truffle oil on top if you want to be fancy.

MAKE IT GLUTEN-FREE: Use gluten-free pasta.

Preheat the oven to 425°F.

On a large rimmed baking sheet, toss the cauliflower and garlic with the olive oil and ½ teaspoon of the salt. Arrange in a single layer and roast for about 30 minutes, or until the cauliflower is very soft, tossing frequently.

Meanwhile, bring a large pot of heavily salted water to a boil over high heat. Add the pasta and cook to al dente according to the package directions. Drain and return the pasta to the pot, off the heat.

Transfer the roasted cauliflower to a blender and add the water, cashews, lemon juice, and remaining 2 teaspoons of salt. Blend on high speed for about 2 minutes, until very smooth. Taste and adjust the seasoning.

Add the sauce to the pot with the pasta and toss to coat. Season with pepper and top with Vegan Parmesan. Serve immediately.

PENNE BROCCOLI ALFREDO CASSEROLE

SERVES 4 TO 6

1 pound **penne**

3 cups (10 ounces) **frozen broccoli florets**

½ cup finely chopped **sun-dried tomatoes**

2 tablespoons **olive oil**

1 large **onion**, chopped

4 **garlic cloves**, minced

1 cup **raw cashews** (see Tip, page 11)

3 cups **water**

2 teaspoons **sea salt**, plus more as needed

½ cup **panko bread crumbs**

Freshly ground **black pepper**

Paprika, for dusting

Casseroles are underappreciated. They are easy, quick, usually save well, and hearty enough to feed an army! Now, why aren't they coming back into style? This particular version is creamy, chock-full-o' broccoli, and lasts for days. Give it a try and I guarantee you'll want to join my casserevolution!

MAKE IT GLUTEN-FREE: Use gluten-free pasta and gluten-free panko bread crumbs.

Preheat the oven to 425°F. Grease a 9 x 13-inch baking dish with cooking spray.

Bring a large pot of heavily salted water to a boil over high heat. Add the pasta and cook to al dente according to the package directions. Just before draining the pasta, add the broccoli and sun-dried tomatoes to the pot and warm for about 30 seconds. Drain and transfer to the prepared baking dish.

Meanwhile, in a medium skillet, heat the olive oil over medium-high heat. When it shimmers, add the onion and garlic and cook for 5 to 7 minutes, until softened. Transfer to a blender. Add the cashews, water, and salt. Blend on high speed for about 2 minutes, until very smooth. Pour the sauce over the noodles and gently toss to coat. Taste and adjust the seasoning.

Top the casserole with the panko, pepper, and paprika and season again with salt. Bake for about 20 minutes, until the top is lightly browned. Serve warm.

SPICY RIGATONI VODKA

SERVES 4 TO 6

1 pound **rigatoni**

2 tablespoons **olive oil**

3 **garlic cloves**, minced

¼ teaspoon **crushed red pepper flakes**, plus more for garnish

1 (28-ounce) can **whole peeled tomatoes**, with their juices

2 teaspoons **sea salt**

2 tablespoons **light brown sugar**

¼ cup **vodka**

½ cup **raw cashews** (see Tip, page 11)

½ cup **water**

If you were ever thinking of going on an exclusive Spicy Rigatoni Vodka diet, you need not look any further. I've tried it and lived to tell the story! It all started when I decided to create this dish because I was craving creamy pasta that wouldn't get boring after the fifth bite. The result was this recipe, and I then made it for myself every day for a whole week. The result? I was generally happier and more pleasant to be around.

MAKE-AHEAD TIP: The sauce can be made in advance and stored in an airtight container in the refrigerator for up to 3 days.

MAKE IT GLUTEN-FREE: Use gluten-free pasta.

Bring a large pot of heavily salted water to a boil over high heat. Add the pasta and cook to al dente according to the package directions. Drain the pasta and return it to the pot, off the heat.

Meanwhile, in a large, deep skillet, heat the olive oil over medium heat. When it shimmers, add the garlic and red pepper flakes and cook for about 1 minute, until fragrant. Carefully stir in the tomatoes and their juices, salt, and brown sugar. Bring to a simmer, stirring occasionally. Add the vodka and simmer for about 5 minutes to let the alcohol burn off.

In a blender, combine the cashews and water. Blend on high speed for about 2 minutes, until very smooth. Carefully add the tomato mixture to the blender and blend again until smooth (be careful when blending hot liquids). Add the sauce to the pot with the pasta and toss to coat. Taste and adjust the seasoning. Top each serving with a pinch of red pepper flakes.

SRIRACHA TEMPEH ALFREDO

SERVES 4 TO 6

1 pound **fettuccine**

cashew sauce

1 tablespoon **olive oil**

1 **onion**, chopped

4 **garlic cloves**, minced

1 cup **raw cashews** (see Tip, page 11)

2 cups **water**

2 tablespoons **sriracha**

1 tablespoon **pure maple syrup**

2 teaspoons **sea salt**

sriracha tempeh

2 tablespoons **olive oil**

8 ounces **tempeh**, cut into bite-size cubes

¼ cup **water**, plus more as needed

2 tablespoons **sriracha**

2 tablespoons **pure maple syrup**

½ teaspoon **sea salt**

Freshly ground **black pepper**

Toppings: Chopped **fresh cilantro**; **lime** wedges

Just days after my boyfriend, Ben, announced that he hated tempeh (cue my heart breaking), I made this pasta for myself and happen to leave the leftovers out on the counter. Ben wandered into the kitchen, and when I looked over, he was eating it straight from the pot, not knowing it had tempeh, and saying it was one of my best pastas yet. Come one, come all, tempeh-lovers, tempeh-haters . . . you are going to *love* this recipe.

MAKE IT GLUTEN-FREE: Use gluten-free pasta.

Bring a large pot of heavily salted water to a boil over high heat. Add the pasta and cook to al dente according to the package directions. Drain the pasta and return it to the pot, off the heat.

Make the cashew sauce: In a medium skillet, heat the olive oil over medium-high heat. Add the onion and garlic and cook for 5 to 7 minutes, until softened. Transfer to a blender; set the skillet aside (no need to wash it). Add the cashews, water, sriracha, maple syrup, and salt to the blender. Blend on high speed for about 2 minutes, until very smooth.

Make the sriracha tempeh: In the same skillet in which you cooked the onion, heat the olive oil over medium-high heat. When it shimmers, add the tempeh and cook, stirring, for 6 to 8 minutes, until golden and lightly browned.

In a small bowl, whisk together the water, sriracha, maple syrup, and salt. Pour the mixture over the tempeh and reduce the heat to medium. Simmer for about 10 minutes, stirring often, until the sauce has somewhat been absorbed and has thickened.

Add the cashew sauce to the pot with the pasta and toss to coat. Season with pepper; taste and adjust the seasoning. If the sauce gets too thick, add water, 1 tablespoon at a time, until the desired consistency is reached. Serve the pasta in bowls and top each serving with the sriracha tempeh, cilantro, and a lime wedge.

CHEESY KELP NOODLES

SERVES 2

12 to 16 ounces **kelp noodles**, drained

¾ cup **raw cashews** (see Tip, page 11)

¾ cup **water**

1 tablespoon **nutritional yeast flakes**

1 tablespoon **lemon juice**

1 tablespoon **pure maple syrup**

2 teaspoons **mellow white miso paste**

1 teaspoon **tamari**

1 teaspoon **sea salt**

¼ teaspoon **ground turmeric**

Pinch of **cayenne pepper**

Vegan Parmesan (page 55)

Smoked paprika, for dusting

Freshly ground **black pepper**

I once read a tweet that said the least interesting thing about a woman is her weight (amen!). Well, I like to say the least interesting thing about a dish is its calorie count—but just for the sake of a fun fact, 12 ounces of kelp noodles have only 18 calories. That's basically like eating air! Kelp noodles come vacuum-packed and can be found in the Asian or pasta aisle of the grocery store. And I promise, this recipe is maximally healthy but just as comforting as good old-fashioned mac and cheese.

MAKE-AHEAD TIP: The sauce can be made in advance and stored in an airtight container in the refrigerator for up to 3 days.

MAKE IT GLUTEN-FREE: Use gluten-free tamari.

Place the noodles in a large bowl and cover with very hot water. Soak for about 10 minutes, until soft. Drain, then rinse with water and drain again. Repeat this a few times to thoroughly "wash" the noodles until the water runs clear. Using kitchen scissors, cut the noodles to the desired length.

Meanwhile, in a blender, combine the cashews, water, nutritional yeast, lemon juice, maple syrup, miso, tamari, salt, turmeric, and cayenne and blend on high speed for about 2 minutes, until very smooth. Transfer the sauce to a medium saucepan and set it over medium-low heat.

Add the soaked noodles to the pot of sauce and heat, stirring occasionally, for about 10 minutes, until the noodles are very soft and warm. Taste and adjust the seasoning. I like my kelp noodles very saucy, but if you prefer less sauce, strain some out. Portion into bowls and top with Vegan Parmesan, smoked paprika, and black pepper.

FIESTA MAC & CHEESE
SERVES 6 TO 8

1 pound elbow **macaroni**

1 (15-ounce) can **kidney beans** or **black beans**, drained and rinsed

1 cup (4 ounces) **frozen sweet yellow corn**, thawed

2 cups **water**

2 cups **raw cashews** (see Tip, page 11)

2 tablespoons **nutritional yeast flakes**

2 tablespoons **agave nectar**

2½ teaspoons **sea salt**

1 teaspoon **smoked paprika**, plus more for garnish

½ teaspoon **ground turmeric**

¼ teaspoon **cayenne pepper**

1 (14.5-ounce) can **diced tomatoes**, with their juices

2 **jalapeños**, seeded and chopped

Chopped **fresh chives**, for garnish

Lime wedges, for serving

This recipe is hearty with a capital H! It's kind of like a cross between tacos and mac and cheese—make it for your hungriest friends and family members and dare them to say vegan food isn't filling! The first time my roommate and I made this, afterward, we were so full that we said we would never eat again. Obviously, the next night, we craved it and made it again!

MAKE IT GLUTEN-FREE: Use gluten-free pasta.

Bring a large pot of heavily salted water to a boil over high heat. Add the pasta and cook to al dente according to the package directions. Place the beans and corn in a large colander in the sink. Drain the pasta on top of the beans and corn, and return everything to the pot.

Meanwhile, in a blender, combine the water, cashews, nutritional yeast, agave, salt, smoked paprika, turmeric, and cayenne. Blend on high speed for about 2 minutes, until very smooth. Add the cashew sauce, tomatoes with their juices, and jalapeños to the pot with the noodles. Cook over medium-low heat for about 5 minutes, until the sauce thickens. If the sauce gets too thick, add water, 1 tablespoon at a time, until the desired consistency is reached.

Top each serving with chives and smoked paprika and serve with a lime wedge.

TAKEOUT SESAME NOODLES

SERVES 2

8 to 10 ounces **udon** or **soba noodles**

3 tablespoons **toasted sesame oil**

¼ cup **tamari**

¼ cup **seasoned rice vinegar**

3 tablespoons **peanut butter**

2 tablespoons **light brown sugar**

1 tablespoon minced **fresh ginger**

Half a **garlic clove**

2 teaspoons **sriracha**, plus more to taste

Toppings: Chopped roasted **peanuts**; thinly sliced **scallions**; **sesame seeds**

I love making this dish for company because it is impressive, full of flavor, and tastes exactly like Chinese cold sesame noodles but is so much healthier. I like to eat it at room temp or even chilled, because I can prep it in advance and not have to worry about heating it up—plus, it's more authentic to the takeout original. But if you can't wait, it's delicious warm, too.

MAKE IT GLUTEN-FREE: Use gluten-free noodles and gluten-free tamari.

Bring a large pot of heavily salted water to a boil over high heat. Add the noodles and cook according to the package directions. Drain and rinse with cold water. Transfer noodles to a large bowl.

Meanwhile, in a blender or food processor, combine the sesame oil, tamari, vinegar, peanut butter, brown sugar, ginger, garlic, and sriracha. Blend until smooth. Add more sriracha, to taste, if desired.

Add the sauce to the pot with the noodles. Toss to coat; taste and adjust the seasoning. Top each serving with peanuts, scallions, and sesame seeds.

BUTTERNUT MAC

SERVES 6

About 5 cups (20 ounces) peeled and cubed **butternut squash**

2 tablespoons **olive oil**

2¼ teaspoons **sea salt**

Freshly ground **black pepper**

1 pound **elbow macaroni**

2 cups **water**, plus more as needed

½ cup **raw cashews** (see Tip, page 11)

1 **garlic clove**

½ teaspoon **dried rosemary**

Toppings: **Smoky Shiitake Bacon** (recipe follows) and **smoked paprika**

This mac-and-cheese recipe was born from my deep love for both roasted butternut squash and mac and cheese. When I discovered that sweet, salty, buttery butternut lends itself so perfectly to a silky cheese sauce, I realized my prayers for nondairy cheese had been answered. A dash of dried rosemary adds a sophisticated, aromatic layer of flavor.

MAKE-AHEAD TIP: The sauce can be made in advance and stored in an airtight container in the refrigerator for up to 3 days.

MAKE IT GLUTEN-FREE: Use gluten-free pasta.

To roast the butternut squash, preheat the oven to 400°F. On a small rimmed baking sheet, toss the squash with the olive oil, ¼ teaspoon of the salt, and season with pepper. Roast for about 30 minutes, until fork tender, turning occasionally with a spatula during baking.

Bring a large pot of heavily salted water to a boil over high heat. Add the pasta and cook to al dente according to the package directions. Drain the pasta and return it to the pot, off the heat.

In a blender, combine the roasted butternut squash, water, cashews, garlic, rosemary, and remaining 2 teaspoons of salt. Blend on high speed for about 2 minutes, until very smooth. Add the sauce to the pot with the pasta and toss to coat. Taste and adjust the seasoning. If the sauce is too thick, add water, 1 tablespoon at a time, until the desired consistency is reached. Top each serving with Smoky Shiitake Bacon and dust with smoked paprika.

recipe continues

smoky shiitake bacon

MAKES ABOUT ½ CUP

About 1 cup (4 ounces) **shiitake mushrooms**, de-stemmed and thinly sliced (about ¼ inch thick)

2 tablespoons **olive oil**

¼ teaspoon **sea salt**, plus more as needed

¼ teaspoon **smoked paprika**

¼ teaspoon **garlic powder**

Preheat the oven to 375°F.

On a large rimmed baking sheet, toss the mushrooms with the olive oil and salt. Arrange the mushrooms in a single layer. Bake for 20 to 30 minutes, turning occasionally with a spatula, until lightly browned and very crisp. Remove from oven and toss with the smoked paprika and garlic powder. Season with salt to taste. Store in an airtight container at room temperature for up to 3 days.

fork it

BOWLS &
PLATED DISHES

BEANS & GREENS WITH SCALLION BISCUITS

SERVES 4 TO 6

beans & greens

2 tablespoons **olive oil**

1 **onion**, diced

1 **green bell pepper**, diced

½ teaspoon **sea salt**

3 cups (about 9 ounces) chopped **collard green leaves**

2 **garlic cloves**, minced

1 tablespoon **ground cumin**

1 teaspoon **chili powder**

½ teaspoon **ground cinnamon**

¼ teaspoon **cayenne pepper**

2 (15-ounce) cans **black-eyed peas** or **red kidney beans**, drained and rinsed

1 (15-ounce) can **tomato sauce**

1 cup **water**

¼ cup **tamari**

¼ cup packed **light brown sugar**

2 tablespoons **apple cider vinegar**

This Southern-style dish is saucy, sweet, and not too spicy. I love eating it over rice and always find myself going back for more and more. Super nourishing, it feels light and healthy but full of flavor. Oh, and do yourself a favor and serve it with Scallion Biscuits and Maple Butter. You're welcome in advance.

MAKE-AHEAD TIP: The biscuit dough can be made in advance and stored wrapped in plastic in the refrigerator for up to 3 days.

MAKE IT GLUTEN-FREE: Use gluten-free tamari and gluten-free baking flour in the biscuits.

Preheat the oven to 375°F.

Make the beans and greens: In a large saucepan, heat the olive oil over medium-high heat. When it shimmers, add the onion, bell pepper, and salt and cook for 5 to 7 minutes, until the onion is nicely browned. Add the collard greens, garlic, cumin, chili powder, cinnamon, and cayenne and sauté for about 3 minutes, until fragrant and the collards are just wilted.

Stir in the black-eyed peas, tomato sauce, water, tamari, brown sugar, and vinegar. Reduce the heat to medium. Simmer for 10 to 15 minutes. Taste and adjust the seasoning.

Make the scallion biscuits: In a food processor, combine the flour, baking powder, and salt and pulse gently until the ingredients are just combined. Add the chilled margarine and pulse again until the mixture has the texture of coarse meal with a few larger margarine lumps. Add the almond milk and pulse a few more times until just combined. Do not overwork the dough. Fold in the scallions by hand.

scallion biscuits

2 cups all-purpose **flour**, plus more for dusting

1 tablespoon **baking powder**

¾ teaspoon **sea salt**

½ cup **vegan margarine**, chilled, plus melted margarine for brushing

¾ cup **almond milk**

⅓ cup thinly sliced **scallions**

Steamed rice, for serving

Whipped Maple Butter (recipe follows), for serving

Transfer the dough to a lightly floured surface and pat it into an oblong shape about 1 inch thick. Using a floured round cookie or biscuit cutter, cut out biscuits and place them on a baking sheet. (Alternatively, scoop out about ¼-cup portions of the dough onto the baking sheet and press them gently with your hands into biscuit shapes.) Brush the tops lightly with melted margarine and bake for about 15 minutes, until lightly golden. Remove from the oven and brush again with melted margarine.

Serve the beans and greens in bowls over rice with warm biscuits and Whipped Maple Butter on the side.

whipped maple butter

MAKES 1¼ CUPS

1 cup **vegan margarine**, at room temperature

¼ cup **pure maple syrup**

In a medium bowl using a whisk or handheld mixer, whip together the margarine and the maple syrup until light and fluffy. Serve immediately or refrigerate for up to 1 week.

PANEER TIKKA MASALA

SERVES 4

½ cup **raw cashews** (see Tip, page 11)

½ cup **water**, plus more as needed

2 tablespoons **vegetable** or **coconut oil**

1 **onion**, chopped

1 **red** or **green bell pepper**, diced

1 (16-ounce) package **extra-firm tofu**, pressed (see Tip, page 14) and cut into ½-inch cubes

4 **garlic cloves**, minced

4 teaspoons minced **fresh ginger**

1 tablespoon **curry powder**

2 tablespoons **tomato paste**

¼ teaspoon **crushed red pepper flakes**

1½ teaspoons **sea salt**

1 (15-ounce) can **diced tomatoes**, with their juices

2 tablespoons **light brown sugar**

Steamed **basmati rice**, for serving

Toppings: Chopped **fresh cilantro**; **lime** wedges

I took my first trip to India to be a bridesmaid in my best friend Ritu's wedding. Ritu and I met in college at Berkeley and then moved to take on New York together right afterward—she to go to law school at Columbia and I to go to culinary school at the Natural Gourmet Institute. Her wedding was a beautiful and filling weeklong affair complete with hot Indian buffets for every meal (and a massive amount of dancing in between meals!). But what was I craving the minute I landed back in New York? More curry! I whipped up this recipe just days after returning home, in memory of my amazing trip.

In a blender, combine the cashews and water. Blend on high speed for about 2 minutes, until very smooth.

In a large nonstick skillet, heat the oil over medium-high heat. When it shimmers, add the onion and bell pepper and cook for 5 to 7 minutes, until the onion is translucent. Add the tofu, garlic, ginger, curry powder, tomato paste, red pepper flakes, and salt and cook for about 3 minutes more, until fragrant. Add the diced tomatoes and their juices and the brown sugar and cook for about 5 minutes, until the flavors come together.

Turn off the heat and stir in the cashew cream. Taste and adjust the seasoning. If the sauce gets too thick, add water to thin it, 1 tablespoon at a time. Spoon over rice and garnish each serving with cilantro and a lime wedge.

CHINESE EGGPLANT WITH SPICY GARLIC SAUCE

SERVES 4

⅓ cup **water**

2 tablespoons **tamari**

2 tablespoons **seasoned rice vinegar**

2 tablespoons **pure maple syrup**

4 **garlic cloves**, minced

1½ teaspoons **sriracha**

¼ teaspoon **crushed red pepper flakes**

1 teaspoon **cornstarch**

2 tablespoons **vegetable oil**

3 long **Asian eggplants** or 1 **American eggplant**, cut into bite-size cubes

2 **scallions**, thinly sliced, plus more for garnish

Steamed rice, for serving

Sesame seeds, for garnish

It had been a while since I had seen my friends Ethan and Raina (also both busy entrepreneurs), so I invited them over for dinner to catch up. I served this dish and they both went back for seconds and thirds. I assumed they were eggplant lovers until Raina reminded me that she actually *hates* eggplant! I obviously had forgotten that when I was menu planning (oops!), but it made it even more exciting that she genuinely loved this dish. Note to self: Never let so much time pass between seeing friends that you forget their food preferences!

MAKE IT GLUTEN-FREE: Use gluten-free tamari.

In a small bowl, whisk together the water, tamari, vinegar, maple syrup, garlic, sriracha, red pepper flakes, and cornstarch until the cornstarch has dissolved.

In a large nonstick skillet, heat the oil over medium-high heat. When it shimmers, add the eggplant and scallions. Cook, stirring often, for about 10 minutes, until the eggplant is nicely browned.

Add the sauce to the pan and reduce the heat to medium. Cook for 10 to 15 minutes, until the eggplant is soft and the sauce is thick. Taste and adjust the seasoning. Serve over rice. Garnish with scallions and sesame seeds.

BURNT GARLIC
UN-FRIED RICE

SERVES 4

4 tablespoons **vegetable oil**, plus more as needed

8 ounces **extra-firm tofu**, drained and crumbled

1 teaspoon **curry powder**

½ teaspoon **ground coriander**

¼ teaspoon **ground turmeric**

1 teaspoon **sea salt**

20 **garlic cloves**, minced or thinly sliced

1 small **onion**, thinly sliced

1 teaspoon minced **fresh ginger**

3 cups cooked **jasmine rice**

½ cup **cashews**

2 **scallions**, thinly sliced

2 teaspoons **lime juice**

Toppings: **Hot sauce** or **sriracha** (optional); **lime** wedges (not optional!)

Dear Garlic,
How can you be so good, even when you're burnt? I'll be wondering.
Love always,
Chloe

While twenty cloves of garlic might sound like a lot, the flavor is pretty mellow and you'll be glad you used every last one. For a shortcut, buy peeled garlic cloves and mince them by pulsing in a food processor.

In a small skillet, heat 1 tablespoon of the oil over medium-high heat. When it shimmers, add the tofu, curry powder, coriander, turmeric, and ½ teaspoon of the salt. Cook, stirring often, for 3 to 5 minutes, until the spices are evenly distributed. Remove the skillet from the heat.

Meanwhile, in a large nonstick skillet or wok, heat the remaining 3 tablespoons of oil over medium-high heat. When it shimmers, add 2 tablespoons of the minced garlic and cook until very browned but not blackened, about 3 minutes. Transfer the burnt garlic to paper towels to drain, reserving the oil in the skillet.

Add the onion to the garlic oil in the skillet and cook over medium-high heat, stirring occasionally, for 5 to 7 minutes, until softened. Season with the remaining ½ teaspoon of salt. Add the ginger, rice, cashews, scallions, and lime juice, and cook, stirring often and adding more oil as needed if the pan looks dry, 6 to 8 minutes more, until heated through.

Stir in the burnt garlic, remaining garlic, and the tofu and cook for about 1 minute more to warm through. Taste and adjust the seasoning. Serve with hot sauce, if desired, and lime wedges.

CALIFORNIA NACHOS

SERVES 6

1 large bag **tortilla chips**

1 (15-ounce) can **black beans**, drained and rinsed

2 tablespoons **olive oil**

8 ounces **ground seitan** (see Tip, page 31)

1 tablespoon **taco seasoning**

½ teaspoon **smoked paprika**

½ teaspoon **chipotle powder**

Sea salt

1 **avocado**, diced

2 teaspoons **lime juice**

Cashew Queso (page 119)

optional toppings

½ cup **fresh tomato salsa**

Lime Sour Cream (page 36)

Finely chopped **red cabbage**

Thinly sliced **jalapeño**

Chopped **fresh cilantro**

Pickled Red Onion (page 115)

Nachos were always a staple in my family since I grew up in Southern California. The Mexican-American side of my family gives this vegan version five stars and said they like the Cashew Queso better than real cheese! My friend Ann Marie served this recipe to her family and told me "their eyes popped out of their heads when I put the platter in front of them!" So there you have it. These nachos are approved, several times over.

MAKE IT GLUTEN-FREE: Use gluten-free tortilla chips and replace the seitan with tempeh.

Preheat the oven to 425°F.

Pile the chips into a 9 x 13-inch baking dish. Add the black beans. Bake for 10 to 15 minutes, until the beans are warmed through.

Meanwhile, in a large skillet, heat the olive oil over medium heat. When it shimmers, add the seitan, taco seasoning, smoked paprika, and chipotle powder and cook for about 5 minutes, until the seitan is heated through. Add water as needed if the skillet seems dry. Season with salt. Remove the skillet from the heat.

In a small bowl, mash together the avocado and lime juice. Season with salt.

Remove the baking dish from the oven and add the Cashew Queso. Scatter over the seitan. Top off the nachos with the mashed avocado and any additional toppings you desire. Serve immediately.

FIREHOUSE CHILI WITH CORNBREAD MUFFINS

SERVES 6 TO 8

1 teaspoon **chili powder**

1 teaspoon **paprika**

1 teaspoon **garlic powder**

1 teaspoon **onion powder**

1 teaspoon **oregano**

1 teaspoon **ground cumin**

1 teaspoon freshly ground **black pepper**

2 teaspoons **sea salt**

2 tablespoons **olive oil**

1 large **onion**, diced

1 medium **green bell pepper**, diced

4 **garlic cloves**, minced

1 cup **water**

2 tablespoons **tomato paste**

1 (28-ounce) can **diced tomatoes**, with their juices

2 (15-ounce) cans **red kidney beans**, drained and rinsed

1 tablespoon **brown sugar** or **pure maple syrup**

Optional Toppings: **Lime Sour Cream** (page 36); diced **red onion**; chopped **fresh cilantro**; **lime** wedges

Cornbread Muffins (recipe follows), for serving

Whipped Maple Butter (page 165), for serving

My friend Chris is a New York City firefighter and a great cook, so I was honored when he asked me for a good chili recipe to share with his firefighting friends. I passed this one along and he liked it so much that he now only makes vegan chili. Try this recipe and eat like a hero!

In a small bowl, combine the chili powder, paprika, garlic powder, onion powder, oregano, cumin, black pepper, and salt.

In a large saucepan, heat the olive oil over medium-high heat. When it shimmers, add the onion and bell pepper and cook, stirring frequently, for about 10 minutes, until very soft. Add the garlic and the spice mixture and cook for about 1 minute more, until fragrant.

Add the water, tomato paste, diced tomatoes with their juices, kidney beans, and brown sugar. Reduce the heat to medium and cook, stirring often, for about 15 minutes, until the flavors come together.

If desired, top each serving with Lime Sour Cream, red onion, cilantro, and a lime wedge. Serve with Cornbread Muffins and Whipped Maple Butter.

cornbread muffins

MAKES 12 MUFFINS

1 cup all-purpose **flour**

1 cup **cornmeal**

⅔ cup **sugar**

2 teaspoons **baking powder**

½ teaspoon **sea salt**

1 cup **almond milk**

½ cup **vegetable oil**

1 tablespoon **apple cider vinegar**

½ cup **fresh** or **frozen corn kernels**

MAKE IT GLUTEN-FREE: Use gluten-free baking flour.

Preheat the oven to 350°F. Line a 12-cup muffin pan with paper liners and lightly grease the liners with cooking spray.

In a large bowl, whisk together the flour, cornmeal, sugar, baking powder, and salt. In a small bowl, whisk together the almond milk, oil, and vinegar. Add the wet ingredients to the dry and stir to combine. Do not overmix. Fold in the corn.

Fill the prepared muffin pan with the batter, filling each muffin cup about two-thirds of the way full. Bake for about 20 minutes, until golden. Remove from the oven and serve warm.

GENERAL TSO'S TOFU

SERVES 2

tofu

1 (16-ounce) package **extra-firm tofu**, pressed (see Tip, page 14) and cubed

2 tablespoons **tamari**

¼ cup **cornstarch**

stir-fry

¼ cup **pure maple syrup**

2 tablespoons **tamari**

1 tablespoon **sriracha**

Juice of 1 **orange**

1 tablespoon **cornstarch**

2 tablespoons **vegetable oil**, plus more as needed

4 **scallions**, cut into ¾-inch pieces

2 large strips of **orange zest**, removed with a vegetable peeler

2 **garlic cloves**, minced

2 teaspoons minced **fresh ginger**

Steamed rice and/or **broccoli**, for serving

Sesame seeds, for garnish

The day I was first experimenting with this recipe, my handyman was over at my apartment fixing a light. The aroma wafted up his ladder, and he couldn't help but ask to taste it. We ended up sharing, and I'm not sure he even knew it was tofu! Add more sriracha if you like it extra spicy. Otherwise, sit back and enjoy the sticky sweet goodness!

MAKE IT GLUTEN-FREE: Use gluten-free tamari.

Make the tofu: In a large zip-top bag, combine the tofu, tamari, and cornstarch. Toss to coat—the cornstarch will become goopy.

Make the stir-fry: In a small bowl, whisk together the maple syrup, tamari, sriracha, orange juice, and cornstarch until the cornstarch has dissolved.

In a large nonstick skillet, heat the oil over medium-high heat. When it shimmers, add the tofu, working in batches as needed, and sear for about 3 minutes on each side, until crispy all over. Add more oil between batches as needed. Return all the tofu to the skillet and add the scallions, orange zest, garlic, and ginger. Cook for about 3 minutes, until the scallions begin to break down. Add the sauce and reduce the heat to low. Cook for about 5 minutes more, until the sauce thickens.

Serve over rice, garnished with sesame seeds.

 **CRISP TOFU**

The key to having crispy tofu cubes is to not flip them over too soon. Let each piece get nicely browned before flipping it to the other side.

HOLIDAY CASHEW NUT ROAST WITH COUNTRY GRAVY

SERVES 6 TO 8

3 tablespoons **olive oil**, plus more for greasing and drizzling

1 **onion**, diced

1 **carrot**, diced

1 cup diced **celery**

¼ cup **cashews**

½ teaspoon **sea salt**

½ teaspoon freshly ground **black pepper**

4 cloves **garlic**, minced

1 teaspoon **dried rosemary**

1 teaspoon **dried thyme**

½ teaspoon **onion powder**

1 (8-ounce) package **tempeh**, crumbled

2½ cups (8 ounces) mixed **mushrooms** (cremini, shiitake, oyster, etc.)

¼ cup **tamari**

2 tablespoons **pure maple syrup**

¾ cup cooked **brown rice**

½ cup **bread crumbs**

½ cup **vegetable broth**

This is a perfect meal for Thanksgiving, Christmas, Hanukkah, my birthday on October 14th—basically any day in fall or winter! It's great to make for a large crowd and transports well, too, if you're on potluck duty. Merry vegan cooking!

MAKE-AHEAD TIP: The roast can be prepped in advance and stored unbaked, covered in plastic, in the refrigerator for up to 2 days. Bake directly from refrigerator.

MAKE IT GLUTEN-FREE: Use gluten-free tamari, gluten-free bread crumbs, gluten-free broth, and gluten-free baking flour.

Preheat the oven to 400°F. Lightly grease an 8-inch square baking dish with olive oil.

In a large skillet, heat 2 tablespoons of the olive oil over medium-high heat. When it shimmers, add the onion, carrot, celery, cashews, salt, and pepper. Cook for about 10 minutes, until nicely browned. Add the garlic, rosemary, thyme, and onion powder, and cook for about 1 minute more, until fragrant.

Transfer the cashew mixture to a food processor, reserving the skillet for later use. Pulse until just combined, then transfer to a large bowl.

Meanwhile, heat the remaining tablespoon of olive oil in the reserved skillet over medium-high heat. When it shimmers, add the tempeh and mushrooms and let cook for about 6 to 8 minutes, adding more oil if needed, until soft and lightly browned. Add the tamari and maple syrup, and let simmer over medium-low heat for about 5 minutes.

recipe continues

country gravy

2 tablespoons **olive oil**

1 **onion**, roughly chopped

¼ cup **nutritional yeast flakes**

¼ cup all-purpose **flour**

2 cups **vegetable broth** or **water**, plus more as needed

1 tablespoon **tamari**

1 **garlic clove**, minced

1 teaspoon **dried rosemary**

Sea salt and freshly ground **black pepper**

Quick Cranberry Sauce (recipe follows) or store-bought cranberry sauce

Add the tempeh mixture to the large bowl and add the brown rice, bread crumbs, and broth. Let sit until cool to the touch, then mix using your hands until well combined. Taste and adjust the seasoning.

Transfer the mixture to the prepared baking dish and firmly pat it down. Lightly brush or drizzle the top of the mixture with olive oil. Bake for about 15 minutes, or until the top is nicely browned.

Meanwhile, make the country gravy: In a medium saucepan, heat the olive oil over medium-high heat. When it shimmers, add the onion and cook, stirring occasionally, for 5 to 7 minutes, until softened. Add the nutritional yeast and flour, and cook, stirring, for about 1 minute to coat the onion with the dry mixture. Add the broth, tamari, garlic, and rosemary and stir to combine—the mixture will be very lumpy. Cook for about 3 minutes more, until the mixture is very thick.

Transfer the gravy to a blender or food processor and puree until smooth (be careful when blending hot liquids). Return the gravy to the pot and season with salt and pepper. Keep warm over low heat until ready to serve. If the gravy gets too thick, add a little more broth or water to thin it.

Serve the roast with gravy and cranberry sauce.

quick cranberry sauce

SERVES 6 TO 8

8 ounces (about 2½ cups) **fresh or frozen cranberries**

½ cup packed **light brown sugar**, plus more as needed

¼ teaspoon **ground ginger**

¼ cup **water**

In a medium saucepan, stir together the cranberries, brown sugar, ginger, and water. Bring to a boil over medium heat, then reduce the heat to medium-low. Cook, stirring frequently, for 30 to 35 minutes, or until the cranberries begin to pop and get saucy.

Remove the pot from the heat and add more brown sugar to taste. Let cool, then store in an airtight container in the refrigerator for up to 5 days.

MANGO-GLAZED TEMPEH

SERVES 4

2 tablespoons **vegetable oil**

1 (8-ounce) package **tempeh**, cut into bite-size cubes

Sea salt

1 small **eggplant**, diced

1 **red bell pepper**, cut into large dice

2 teaspoons minced **fresh ginger**

2 **garlic cloves**, minced

½ cup **mango jam** (see Note)

2 tablespoons **sriracha**

2 tablespoons **tamari**

1 tablespoon **pure maple syrup**

Steamed rice, for serving

Mango is one of my favorite fruits to put in savory dishes because its bright flavor can give life to almost any dish. Using mango jam here is a quick way to make a thick, Asian-inspired sauce, so you don't have to thicken it with cornstarch. The addition of eggplant adds juiciness by soaking up the sweet sauce.

NOTE: If you can't find mango jam, use apricot or peach preserves.

MAKE IT GLUTEN-FREE: Use gluten-free tamari.

In a large nonstick skillet, heat the oil over medium-high heat. When it shimmers, add the tempeh. Season with salt and cook for 6 to 8 minutes, until nicely browned on all sides. Add the eggplant and bell pepper and cook, stirring frequently, for about 10 minutes, until soft and browned, adding more oil as needed if the pan looks dry. Add the ginger and garlic and cook for about 1 minute more, until fragrant.

Reduce the heat to medium and add the jam, sriracha, tamari, and maple syrup. Toss to coat. Taste and adjust the seasoning. Serve over rice.

PANANG CURRY

SERVES 4 TO 6

2 tablespoons **vegetable oil**

1 small **sweet potato**, peeled and cut into ½-inch cubes

1 small **onion**, diced

4 **garlic cloves**, minced

1 tablespoon **curry powder**

2 teaspoons **sea salt**

½ teaspoon **cayenne pepper**

¼ cup **tomato paste**

2 cups gluten-free **vegetable broth**

¼ cup **peanut butter**

1 (13.5-ounce) can **coconut milk**

1 (15.5-ounce) can **chickpeas**, drained and rinsed

3 tablespoons **light brown sugar**

Steamed rice, for serving

toppings

Chopped **peanuts**

Chopped **fresh cilantro**

Sliced **chiles** (as hot as you like!)

Lime wedges

Panang curry is one of my favorites because it tastes like a cross between Thai peanut sauce and red curry. This warming, earthy chickpea and sweet potato stew is laced with peanut-buttery goodness and has so many layers of flavor. Plus, it's a great one-pot "make ahead" meal. I like to make it on a Sunday, store leftovers in the refrigerator or freezer, and reheat it throughout the week. Make it greener by wilting in chopped collards, chard, or kale.

In a large saucepan, heat the oil over medium-high heat. When it shimmers, add the sweet potato and onion and cook for about 8 minutes, until the onion is softened. Add the garlic, curry powder, salt, cayenne, and tomato paste and cook for a few minutes more, until fragrant.

Add the broth, cover, and cook for about 10 minutes more, until the sweet potatoes are fork-tender. Add the peanut butter, coconut milk, chickpeas, and brown sugar. Cook for about 5 minutes, until heated through. Taste and adjust the seasoning.

Spoon over rice and garnish with chopped peanuts, cilantro, chiles, and lime wedges.

SEITAN BROCCOLI STIR-FRY IN SPICY CASHEW DRESSING

SERVES 4

spicy cashew sauce

¾ cup **raw cashews** (see Tip, page 11)

¼ cup **water**

¼ cup **pure maple syrup**

2 tablespoons **tamari**

2 tablespoons **lime juice**

2 tablespoons **sriracha**

1 teaspoon minced **fresh ginger**

Half a **garlic clove**, minced

⅛ teaspoon **sea salt**

stir-fry

¼ cup **vegetable broth** or **water**

2 tablespoons **tamari**

1 tablespoon **pure maple syrup**

1 tablespoon **cornstarch**

2 tablespoons **vegetable oil**

8 ounces **seitan** strips

About 3 cups (10 ounces) bite-size **broccoli florets**

Steamed rice, for serving

My friend Deepti and I met on Craigslist to be roommates when I first moved to New York for culinary school. We didn't know each other when we moved in together, but soon began calling each other the "Craigslist Jackpot" thanks to how quickly we became friends. I was constantly testing recipes on her, and we'd talk for hours about food, dating, and New York City life. Fast-forward almost a decade: We don't live together anymore, but I still like to invite her over for taste-testing, now with her vegetarian husband, Bhavin. They both gave this dish two thumbs up. The seitan tastes surprisingly meaty and the spicy cashew sauce is kind of addicting. You can use the spicy cashew sauce on everything (salad, veggies, grains, etc.).

MAKE-AHEAD TIP: The spicy cashew sauce can be made in advance and stored in an airtight container in the refrigerator for up to 3 days.

Make the spicy cashew sauce: In a blender, combine all the sauce ingredients and blend on high speed for about 2 minutes, until completely smooth.

Make the stir-fry: In a small bowl, combine the broth, tamari, maple syrup, and cornstarch and whisk until smooth and the cornstarch has dissolved.

In a large nonstick skillet, heat the oil over medium-high heat. When it shimmers, add the seitan and broccoli and cook, stirring often, for 3 to 5 minutes, until the broccoli softens and turns bright green and the seitan starts to brown. Add the cornstarch mixture and reduce the heat to medium-low. Cook for about 3 minutes more, until the broccoli and seitan are nicely coated with sauce.

Spoon over steamed rice and drizzle (or drown!) each serving with spicy cashew sauce.

THAI RED CURRY BOWL

SERVES 4 TO 6

2 tablespoons **vegetable oil**

1 large **shallot**, thinly sliced

2 **bell peppers** (I use red and yellow), thinly sliced

6 **garlic cloves**, minced

2 teaspoons minced **fresh ginger**

3 tablespoons **vegan red curry paste**

2 teaspoons **sea salt**

2 (13.5-ounce) cans **coconut milk**

1 (16-ounce) package **extra-firm tofu**, pressed (see Tip, page 14) and cubed

1 (8-ounce) can **bamboo shoots**, drained

2 tablespoons **light brown sugar**

2 tablespoons **lime juice**

Handful of **fresh Thai basil leaves** (or regular basil), leaves torn

Steamed rice, for serving

Toppings: Toasted **cashews**; **lime** wedges

My friend Daniella is also a vegan chef—we met through the Natural Gourmet Institute. We soon became friends, then roommates, and now everyone thinks we're sisters! Well, we have one common weakness: red curry tofu takeout from our local Thai spot. Yes, even chefs crave takeout—we actually love this dish so much we dream about it. We decided that as chefs, we had to crack the code to replicate the dish ourselves. For a straight month we made Thai red curry every single night until it was indiscernible from "the real thing."

In a large saucepan, heat the oil over medium-high heat. When it shimmers, add the shallot and bell peppers and cook for about 5 minutes, until softened. Add the garlic, ginger, curry paste, and salt and cook for about 3 minutes more, until fragrant. Add the coconut milk, tofu, bamboo shoots, brown sugar, and lime juice. Cook over medium heat for about 3 minutes, until heated through.

Add the basil, taste, and adjust the seasoning. Spoon over rice and garnish each serving with cashews and a lime wedge.

VEGAN RAMEN BOWL

SERVES 4

About 8 ounces **dried ramen noodles**

3 tablespoons **vegetable oil**, plus more as needed

1 (16-ounce) package **extra-firm tofu**, pressed (see Tip, page 14) and cubed

¼ cup **hoisin sauce**

2½ cups (8 ounces) **shiitake mushrooms**, sliced

1 bunch **baby bok choy**, coarsely chopped

2 **garlic cloves**, minced

1 teaspoon **curry powder**

¼ teaspoon **sea salt**

4 cups **vegetable broth**

1 (13.5-ounce) can **coconut milk**

Toppings: Thinly sliced **scallions**; **sesame seeds**; **sriracha** or **chili-garlic sauce** (if you like it spicy!)

My current obsession is the coolest noodle bar in LA: Ramen Hood in Grand Central Market. You guessed it . . . it's *all* vegan. Traditional ramen uses pork, beef, and egg, and even if you find a ramen restaurant with a vegetarian option, there's usually something fishy in the broth. I had to find a way to eat this deliciousness from across the country in New York City. I love the mild, coconutty broth, which adds a milkiness that most varieties of ramen don't have. You can use fresh vegan ramen noodles if your grocery store sells them; otherwise, the dried noodles from a ramen noodle soup pack will do—just throw away the seasoning packet. Or try udon or soba.

MAKE IT GLUTEN-FREE: Use gluten-free noodles, gluten-free hoisin sauce, and gluten-free broth.

Bring a large pot of heavily salted water to a boil over high heat. Add the noodles and cook according to the package directions. Drain and rinse with cold water and return to the pot, off the heat.

Meanwhile, in a large nonstick skillet, heat 2 tablespoons of the oil over medium-high heat. When it shimmers, add the tofu and sear for about 3 minutes on each side, until golden and crispy (see Tip, page 176). Add more oil as needed if the pan looks dry. Add the hoisin sauce, then reduce the heat to low and turn the tofu to coat.

In a large saucepan, heat the remaining tablespoon of vegetable oil over medium-high heat. When it shimmers, add the mushrooms and bok choy and cook, stirring occasionally, for 3 to 5 minutes, until the mushrooms are soft and the bok choy has wilted. Add the garlic, curry powder, and salt and cook for about 1 minute more, until fragrant. Add the broth and bring to a boil, then reduce the heat to low and stir in the coconut milk. Add the cooked ramen noodles and stir until heated through.

Ladle the broth and noodles into bowls and top each serving with scallions, sesame seeds, and tofu. If you like a little heat, add a drizzle of sriracha or a dollop of chili-garlic sauce.

sippin' on...

COCKTAILS, SMOOTHIES & DRINKS

BOOZY ROOT BEER FLOAT

SERVES 1

1 (12-ounce) can or bottle natural **root beer** or **cola**

2 or 3 tablespoons **vodka**

1 scoop **vegan vanilla ice cream**, store-bought or homemade (page 245)

On our first date, Ben picked a beer bar for us to meet. I hated beer, but I was too embarrassed to say so and felt like I had to play it cool. So I ordered the most delicious-sounding beer on the menu, some kind of raspberry beer, hoping I could get it down and blend right in. The good news is that the beer turned out to be sweet and delicious, but the bad news is that it was bright pink, and everyone was staring at me! Lucky for me, the date went well, and while I still don't love beer, Ben and I both love this boozy root beer float—sweet, fizzy, creamy deliciousness. That counts as beer, right?

Stir together the root beer and vodka to taste in a large glass or mug. Add a scoop of ice cream and serve immediately with a straw and spoon.

VEGAN NOG

SERVES 2

1 cup **coconut milk** (use canned for a thicker consistency; see Tip, page 15)

1 cup **almond milk**

2 tablespoons **pure maple syrup**

2 teaspoons **pure vanilla extract**

1 teaspoon **ground cinnamon**, plus more for dusting

½ teaspoon **ground nutmeg**

¼ teaspoon **ground turmeric**

Pinch of **sea salt**

2 to 4 tablespoons **rum** (optional)

Here's my first memory of eggnog: When I was a little girl, I was at a friend's house on a playdate, and her mom served up eggnog out of a carton (nonalcoholic, of course). I had never tried eggnog before, and they were explaining it to me as an "eggy" milk with spices. I wasn't even vegan yet, but something about the concept sounded completely unappealing. Flash-forward to my vegan life, and suddenly the concept of a festive almond-coconut beverage with holiday spice and rum makes perfect sense. A pinch of turmeric gives this drink the faintest "eggy" yellow tint, without the yucky raw egg. Cheers!

MAKE-AHEAD TIP: The nog can be made in advance and stored in an airtight container in the refrigerator for up to 3 days. Stir well and add the rum right before serving.

In a blender, combine the coconut milk, almond milk, maple syrup, vanilla, cinnamon, nutmeg, turmeric, and salt. Blend on high speed for about 1 minute, until smooth.

Fill two whiskey glasses with ice. Add 1 to 2 tablespoons of the rum to each glass, if desired, then top them off with the eggnog mixture. Stir.

Dust each drink with cinnamon and serve.

"I THINK I'M GETTING SICK" CITRUS SHOOTER

SERVES 2

¼ cup fresh **lemon juice**

¼ cup fresh **orange** or **grapefruit juice**

2 tablespoons **fresh ginger juice** (see Note)

Cayenne pepper, for dusting

I make this alkalizing, immune-boosting shooter every time I feel a tickle in my throat, and it works like a charm! If you're already sick, take a shot of this in the morning and you'll be surprisingly cleared up for the day. If you have oil of oregano, a few drops is an incredible addition to prevent and treat infection.

NOTE: To make ginger juice, finely grate fresh ginger using a Microplane, then squeeze the juice out of the pulp using cheesecloth or a nut-milk bag.

Put the lemon, orange, and ginger juices in a spouted container and stir to combine. Pour into shot glasses and dust the tops with cayenne.

MACADAMIA NUT MILK

MAKES 3 CUPS

2 cups **water**

¾ cup **raw macadamia nuts**
(see Tip, page 11)

2 tablespoons **pure maple
syrup**

2 teaspoons **pure vanilla
extract**

Pinch of **sea salt**

Move over almond and coconut—macadamia is the new "it" milk in town! It's creamy and bright white, with a delicious flavor that will take you right to a faraway island. Drink it straight up or add it to your cereal, smoothies, coffee, or lattes. It makes everything taste just a little better.

In a blender, combine the water, macadamia nuts, maple syrup, vanilla, and salt and blend on high speed for about 2 minutes, until very smooth.

For a super-smooth milk, strain through a nut-milk bag. (I don't mind some texture, so I serve it right away.)

Store in an airtight container in the refrigerator for up to 3 days.

MEXICAN HOT CHOCOLATE

SERVES 4

2 cups **almond milk**

½ cup **vegan chocolate chips**

1 tablespoon **creamy peanut butter** or **almond butter**

1 tablespoon **light brown sugar**

1 teaspoon **pure vanilla extract**

½ teaspoon **ground cinnamon**

Pinch of **cayenne pepper** (optional)

Gluten-free vegan marshmallows (see page 17), for serving

Cinnamon sticks, for garnish

This silky hot cocoa is so warming and comforting, it's absolutely perfect for anyone who likes to drink their dessert. The secret ingredient is a touch of nut butter to make it even more creamy than non-vegan hot cocoa.

In a small saucepan, combine the almond milk, chocolate chips, nut butter, brown sugar, vanilla, cinnamon, and cayenne (if using). Warm over medium heat, whisking frequently, for about 3 minutes, until the chocolate has melted and the mixture is smooth.

Remove from the heat, pour into mugs, drop in a few marshmallows, and garnish each serving with a cinnamon stick.

OATMEAL SMOOTHIE

MAKES 2 SMOOTHIES

1 **banana**, chopped and frozen

1 cup **ice**

2 tablespoons **almond butter**

1 cup **almond milk**

1 teaspoon **pure vanilla extract**

½ teaspoon **ground cinnamon**

6 **Medjool dates**, pitted

½ cup **rolled oats**

Feels like oatmeal. Tastes like ice cream. Fuels like breakfast. I especially love this in summer months when I'm in the mood for something cool and refreshing but more substantial than a fruit or veggie smoothie.

MAKE IT GLUTEN-FREE: Use gluten-free oats.

In a blender, combine the banana, ice, almond butter, almond milk, vanilla, and cinnamon and blend until smooth. Add the dates and oats and blend again until mostly smooth, leaving some texture, if desired. Serve immediately in tall glasses.

VANILLA-DATE-MATCHA SMOOTHIE

MAKES 2 SMOOTHIES

1 cup chopped **kale leaves**

1 **banana**, chopped and frozen

1 tablespoon **almond butter**

1 cup **almond milk**

1 cup **ice**

2 teaspoons **pure vanilla extract**

4 **Medjool dates**, pitted

1 teaspoon **matcha green tea powder**

My chef friend Ann Marie has a six-year-old son, Matthew. He eats his veggies from root to stem and has the ability to detect if a baked good is gluten-free just from one sniff! He has his own Instagram account where he rates restaurants, so when Ann Marie and I cook together, we always seek Matthew's approval. You'll be pleased to know that Matthew loves this smoothie and also calls it a milk shake because it tastes so indulgent. Adding vanilla is a great way to make your smoothies taste like dessert without any added calories. If you prefer extra caffeine, double the matcha.

In a blender, combine all the ingredients and blend until smooth. Pour into tall glasses and serve immediately.

ROSEMARY LEMONADE

SERVES 6

½ bunch **fresh rosemary sprigs** (about ½ ounce), plus more for garnish

1 cup **sugar**

5 cups **water**, plus more as needed

1½ cups **fresh lemon juice** (from about 7 lemons)

Lemonade is one of my favorite beverages. I crave it with everything I eat. Making it yourself is an easy way to add an extra-special touch to any meal you're serving. You can infuse it with any herb, but I think there is something especially magical about rosemary because it is so aromatic.

MAKE-AHEAD TIP: The rosemary syrup can be made in advance and stored in the refrigerator in an airtight container for up to 2 days.

In a medium saucepan, combine the rosemary, sugar, and 1 cup of the water. Bring to a boil over medium-high heat, then reduce the heat and simmer, stirring frequently, for about 5 minutes, until fragrant.

Remove the pot from heat and strain the liquid into a pitcher, discarding the rosemary. Let cool completely. Stir in the lemon juice and the remaining 4 cups of water. Taste and add more water as needed.

Chill in the refrigerator and serve in tall glasses over ice. Garnish each glass with a rosemary sprig.

SNOW-DAY MULLED WINE

SERVES 4 TO 6

1 (750-ml) bottle inexpensive **red wine**

3 cups **apple cider**

¼ cup packed **light brown sugar**

2 teaspoons **pure vanilla extract**

1 **orange**, sliced into rounds

2 **cinnamon sticks**, plus more for garnish

Star anise pods, for garnish (optional)

Ever have a super-cheap bottle of red wine in the back of your pantry that you don't know what to do with? Mull it, of course! When I visited my friends Monica and Devang in London, they took me to the outdoor holiday markets, which were filled with stalls selling mulled wine. I sampled quite a few of them for "research." My favorites were the ones with orange slices.

In a large saucepan, combine all the ingredients except the star anise. Simmer over low heat for about 15 minutes, until fragrant.

Ladle into mugs and garnish each with a cinnamon stick and star anise, if desired.

BLOOD ORANGE SANGRIA

SERVES 4

1 (750-ml) bottle inexpensive **red wine**

2 cups **blood orange soda**

2 tablespoons **agave nectar**

Juice of 1 **lime**

2 **blood oranges** (or other oranges), sliced

1 **apple**, finely diced

Fun fact: I'm a vegan chef by day and a matchmaker by night. I get it from my mom, who has made two marriages! Every year around Christmas, we host our annual Singles Mixer. We invite *everyone*—friends, neighbors, our veterinarian, guys we met at the Apple Genius Bar, even shoppers at Whole Foods. We make name tags and play ice-breaker games, and also cook a huge vegan dinner. We always make blood orange sangria to get the conversation flowing and the sparks flying! Add whatever fruit you have in your fridge!

Put all the ingredients in a large pitcher and stir to combine. Serve over ice.

sweet yo'self

DESSERT

CHOCOLATE-AVOCADO CUPCAKES

MAKES 16 CUPCAKES

cupcakes

1½ cups all-purpose **flour**

1 cup **granulated sugar**

⅓ cup **unsweetened cocoa powder**

1 teaspoon **baking soda**

½ teaspoon **sea salt**

1 cup canned **coconut milk**, mixed well (see Tip, page 15)

½ cup **vegetable oil**

2 tablespoons **apple cider vinegar**

2 teaspoons **pure vanilla extract**

½ cup **vegan mini chocolate chips**, plus more for topping

frosting

1 ripe **avocado**

¼ cup **coconut oil** or **vegan margarine**, melted (I like to use unrefined coconut oil for a subtle coconutty flavor)

4 cups **confectioners' sugar**

2 teaspoons **pure vanilla extract**

Almond milk, as needed

My love for avocado is no secret. It's nature's substitute for butter, so why not turn it into frosting? It makes it creamier and richer than usual. If you want a greener color, you can add a touch of matcha green tea powder (about ¼ teaspoon) to the frosting to enhance it. Matcha is expensive, so make the most of your ingredient purchase by checking out my recipes for Vanilla-Date-Matcha Smoothie (page 201) and Matcha Chocolate Chip Muffins (page 45), too!

MAKE-AHEAD TIP: The cupcakes can be made in advance and frozen, unfrosted, for up to 1 month. Thaw and frost before serving.

MAKE IT GLUTEN-FREE: Use gluten-free baking flour, gluten-free cocoa powder, and gluten-free chocolate chips.

Make the cupcakes: Preheat the oven to 350°F. Line two 12-cup muffin pans with 16 cupcake liners.

In a large bowl, whisk together the flour, granulated sugar, cocoa powder, baking soda, and salt. In a medium bowl, whisk together the coconut milk, oil, vinegar, and vanilla. Add the wet ingredients to the dry and whisk until just combined. Do not overmix. Fold in the chocolate chips.

Fill the cupcake liners about two-thirds of the way full with the batter. Bake for 18 to 20 minutes, or until a toothpick inserted into the center of a cupcake comes out clean with a few crumbs clinging to it.

Meanwhile, make the frosting: In a stand mixer fitted with the whisk attachment or in a large bowl using a handheld mixer, beat the avocado and coconut oil until smooth. With the mixer running on low, add the confectioners' sugar and vanilla, and beat to incorporate. Beat on high for about 2 minutes more, until light and fluffy. If needed, add almond milk, 1 teaspoon at a time, to thin.

Let the cupcakes cool completely. Spread or pipe a thin layer of frosting over each cupcake and decorate with mini chocolate chips.

PUMPKIN PIE CUPCAKES

MAKES 16 CUPCAKES

cinnamon whipped cream

1 (13.5-ounce) can **coconut milk** (see Note, page 142), chilled in the refrigerator overnight (be sure not to shake or stir)

¼ cup **confectioners' sugar**

¼ teaspoon **ground cinnamon**

cupcakes

2 cups all-purpose **flour**

1 cup **granulated sugar**

1 teaspoon **baking soda**

1 teaspoon **sea salt**

1 tablespoon **pumpkin pie spice**

1 cup canned **pure pumpkin puree**

1 cup canned **coconut milk**, mixed well (see Tip, page 15)

½ cup **vegetable oil**

2 tablespoons **apple cider vinegar**

1 tablespoon **pure vanilla extract**

Perfect for fall and winter, these cupcakes are major showstoppers. Make them for Thanksgiving dessert and no one will miss the pumpkin pie.

MAKE-AHEAD TIP: The cupcakes can be made in advance and frozen, unfrosted, for up to 1 month. Thaw and frost before serving.

MAKE IT GLUTEN-FREE: Use gluten-free baking flour.

Make the whipped cream: Chill the bowl and whisk attachment of a stand mixer in the freezer for about 10 minutes. Skim the solidified coconut cream from the chilled can of coconut milk and transfer the solids to the bowl of the stand mixer. Do not include any of the coconut water, even if you have to leave behind a little margin of coconut cream.

Add the confectioners' sugar and cinnamon and whip for a few minutes, until the mixture begins to stiffen and turn into whipped cream. Transfer the whipped cream to an airtight container and refrigerate for 1 hour or up to overnight.

Meanwhile, make the cupcakes: Preheat the oven to 350°F. Line two 12-cup muffin pans with 16 cupcake liners.

In a large bowl, whisk together the flour, granulated sugar, baking soda, salt, and pumpkin pie spice. In a medium bowl, whisk together the pumpkin puree, coconut milk, oil, vinegar, and vanilla. Add the wet ingredients to the dry and whisk until just combined. Do not overmix.

Fill the cupcake liners about two-thirds of the way full with the batter. Bake for 16 to 20 minutes, or until a toothpick inserted into the center of a cupcake comes out clean with a few crumbs clinging to it.

When the cupcakes have cooled, spread or pipe a small dollop of whipped cream over each cupcake.

COOKIE DOUGH TRUFFLES

MAKES ABOUT 45 TRUFFLES

½ cup **vegan margarine**

¾ cup packed **light brown sugar**

¼ teaspoon **sea salt**

1 tablespoon **pure vanilla extract**

2 tablespoons **water**

1¼ cups all-purpose **flour**

⅓ cup **vegan mini chocolate chips**

2 cups **vegan chocolate chips**

Cookie dough eaters—you know who you are. I, too, have made countless batches of dough that never made it into the oven. But the best part about vegan baking is that it's always safe to eat the cookie dough straight-up because it is egg-free. Here I've taken bite-size mounds of cookie dough and dipped them into warm semisweet chocolate. Try these once and you may never want to bake your cookies again.

MAKE-AHEAD TIP: The truffles can be made in advance and frozen for up to 1 month.

Line two rimmed baking sheets with parchment paper.

In a stand mixer fitted with the whisk attachment or in a large bowl using a handheld mixer, beat together the margarine, brown sugar, salt, vanilla, and water until combined. Add the flour and beat until incorporated. Fold in the mini chocolate chips by hand. Cover the dough and refrigerate for about 1 hour, until firm.

Roll the chilled dough into 1-inch balls with the palms of your hands. Place on the prepared baking sheets. Freeze for at least 15 minutes, until firm.

Meanwhile, in the top of a double boiler, melt the regular-size chocolate chips, then let cool to room temperature. (Alternatively, put the chocolate chips in a small microwave-safe bowl and microwave in 15-second intervals, stirring after each, until melted and smooth.) Remove one sheet of cookie dough balls from the freezer. Drop each ball into the melted chocolate and remove using two forks, allowing the excess to drip off. Return the coated balls to the baking sheet and transfer to the refrigerator. Repeat with the second sheet of cookie dough balls. Chill for about 20 minutes, until the chocolate is set. Keep refrigerated until ready to serve.

EVERYTHING COOKIES

MAKES ABOUT 15 COOKIES

2¼ cups all-purpose **flour**

1 tablespoon **cornstarch**

1 teaspoon **baking soda**

¾ teaspoon **sea salt**

1 cup **vegan margarine**

1 cup packed **light brown sugar**

½ cup **granulated sugar**

3 tablespoons **water**

1 tablespoon **pure vanilla extract**

½ cup **vegan chocolate chips**, plus more for topping

½ cup **shredded coconut**

½ cup **rolled oats**

½ cup **sweetened dried cranberries** or **cherries**

I love chocolate chip cookies, but I also love oatmeal cookies and coconut cookies and cranberry cookies, so I combined them all together into the ultimate vegan "kitchen sink"–style cookie. If you can think of a cookie ingredient that I left out, by all means add it! Also, these cookies are huge—which isn't a bad thing . . .

MAKE-AHEAD TIP: The cookie dough can be made in advance, scooped, and frozen, for up to 1 month. If baking directly from frozen, you may need to increase the baking time.

MAKE IT GLUTEN-FREE: Use gluten-free baking flour, gluten-free chocolate chips, and gluten-free oats.

Preheat the oven to 350°F. Line two large baking sheets with parchment paper.

In a medium bowl, whisk together the flour, cornstarch, baking soda, and salt.

In a stand mixer fitted with the whisk attachment or in a large bowl using a handheld mixer, beat together the margarine, brown sugar, granulated sugar, water, and vanilla about 2 minutes, until fluffy. Slowly beat in the flour mixture until incorporated. Fold in the chocolate chips, coconut, oats, and cranberries by hand.

Scoop about ¼-cup portions of the dough onto the prepared baking sheets, leaving about 3 inches between each. Top each with more chocolate chips. Bake for about 18 minutes, or until the edges are golden. Let the cookies cool on the baking sheets before serving.

MINT CHOCOLATE CRINKLE COOKIES

MAKES ABOUT 18 COOKIES

1 cup all-purpose **flour**

½ cup **unsweetened cocoa powder**

½ teaspoon **sea salt**

1 cup packed **light brown sugar**

¼ cup **vegan margarine**

⅓ cup **applesauce**

2 teaspoons **pure peppermint extract**

¾ cup **vegan chocolate chips**, melted and cooled (see page 213)

½ cup **granulated sugar**

½ cup **confectioners' sugar**, plus more for dusting

These cute little cookies are super festive at the holidays with their snowy confectioners' sugar tops. If you don't love peppermint and chocolate (*Who are you?!*), you can omit the mint extract for plain chocolate cookies.

MAKE-AHEAD TIP: The cookie dough can be made in advance, scooped, and frozen, for up to 1 month. If baking directly from frozen, you may need to increase the baking time.

MAKE IT GLUTEN-FREE: Use gluten-free baking flour, gluten-free cocoa powder, and gluten-free chocolate chips.

Preheat the oven to 350°F. Line a large baking sheet with parchment paper.

In a medium bowl, whisk together the flour, cocoa powder, and salt.

In a stand mixer fitted with the whisk attachment or in a large bowl using a handheld mixer, beat the brown sugar, margarine, applesauce, and peppermint extract for about 2 minutes, until fluffy. Slowly beat in the flour mixture and melted chocolate until combined.

Place the granulated sugar and confectioners' sugar in separate small bowls. Scoop out about 2 tablespoons of the dough and, using your hands, roll it into a ball. Roll the ball of dough through the granulated sugar until completely coated. Then roll it through the bowl of confectioners' sugar. Place the ball on the prepared baking sheet and repeat with the remaining dough, leaving about 2 inches between each cookie. Bake for about 12 minutes, or until the tops of the cookies look cracked. Let cool on the pan and dust with more confectioners' sugar just before serving.

GLUTEN-FREE ALMOND BUTTER CHOCOLATE CHIP COOKIES

MAKES ABOUT 22 COOKIES

1 cup **gluten-free oat flour**

1 cup **gluten-free baking flour**

½ teaspoon **sea salt**

½ teaspoon **baking soda**

½ teaspoon **xanthan gum**

¾ cup **vegan margarine**

½ cup **granulated sugar**

½ cup packed **light brown sugar**

1 tablespoon **creamy almond butter**

1 tablespoon **pure vanilla extract**

1 to 4 tablespoons **water**

½ cup **vegan gluten-free chocolate chips**, plus more for topping

These are my signature gluten-free cookies, and I actually prefer them to regular cookies. I enjoy the flavor of oat flour, which has subtle nutty, earthy notes that pair beautifully with rich dark chocolate chips. Using two different types of flours prevents either from overpowering the entire flavor of the cookie—so no one can say the cookies taste "gluten-free"! P.S. To make your own oat flour, pulse rolled oats to a fine powder in a food processor. For gluten-free baking flour, I love Bob's Red Mill 1 to 1. It's like gluten-free magic.

MAKE-AHEAD TIP: The cookie dough can be made in advance, scooped, and frozen, for up to 1 month. If baking directly from frozen, you may need to increase the baking time.

Preheat the oven to 350°F. Line two large baking sheets with parchment paper.

In a medium bowl, whisk together the oat flour, baking flour, salt, baking soda, and xanthan gum.

In a stand mixer fitted with the whisk attachment, beat together the margarine, granulated sugar, brown sugar, almond butter, vanilla, and 1 tablespoon of water for about 2 minutes, until fluffy. Slowly beat in the flour mixture until incorporated. If the dough is too dry, beat in 1 or 2 more tablespoons of water, as needed. Fold in the chocolate chips by hand.

Scoop about a 2-tablespoon portion of the dough onto the prepared baking sheets, leaving about 3 inches between each scoop. Top each scoop with more chocolate chips.

Bake for 12 to 13 minutes, or until the edges of the cookies are golden. Remove the baking sheets from the oven. Let the cookies cool on the baking sheets before serving.

SEA SALTED CHOCOLATE CHUNK COOKIES

MAKES ABOUT 14 COOKIES

2¼ cups all-purpose **flour**

1 tablespoon **cornstarch**

1 teaspoon **baking soda**

¾ teaspoon **sea salt**

1 cup **vegan margarine**

1 cup packed **light brown sugar**

¼ cup **agave nectar**

1 tablespoon **pure vanilla extract**

¾ cup **vegan chocolate chunks** or **coarsely chopped chocolate**, plus more for topping

Coarse or **flaky sea salt**, for topping

A little sprinkling of coarse or flaky sea salt lends elegance to what would otherwise be an ordinary chocolate chip cookie. Using chocolate chunks also brings an excitement factor that chocoholics go nuts for! I use a combination of sugar and agave in this recipe because it makes for a softer, chewier cookie.

MAKE-AHEAD TIP: The cookie dough can be made in advance, scooped, and frozen, for up to 1 month. If baking directly from frozen, you may need to increase the baking time.

MAKE IT GLUTEN-FREE: Use gluten-free baking flour and gluten-free chocolate.

Preheat the oven to 350°F. Line a large baking sheet with parchment paper.

In a medium bowl, whisk together the flour, cornstarch, baking soda, and salt.

In a stand mixer fitted with the whisk attachment or in a large bowl using a handheld mixer, beat together the margarine, brown sugar, agave, and vanilla for about 2 minutes, until fluffy. Slowly beat in the flour mixture until incorporated. Fold in the chocolate by hand.

Scoop about ¼-cup portions of the dough onto the prepared baking sheet, leaving about 3 inches between each. Do not flatten. Top them with extra chocolate chunks and sprinkle very lightly with a few grains of the coarse salt on each. Bake for about 15 minutes, or until the edges are golden. (I like the centers slightly undercooked.) Remove the baking sheet from the oven and tap it on the countertop to flatten the cookies a bit. Let cool on the baking sheet before serving.

RASPBERRY SHORTBREAD BARS

MAKES 16 BARS

2 cups all-purpose **flour**

1 cup **vegan margarine**

½ cup **granulated sugar**

½ teaspoon **sea salt**

1 (12- to 18-ounce) jar **raspberry jam**

Confectioners' sugar, for dusting

When I was growing up, my mom used to make me jelly cookies, a combination of shortbread and seeded raspberry jam. We would eat them hot out of the oven and always loved the crust part best. We created these vegan bar cookies together; they have crust on the bottom *and* the top, making the ratio exactly as we love it.

NOTE: These bars are best if chilled in the refrigerator for a few hours or overnight before serving.

MAKE IT GLUTEN-FREE: Use gluten-free baking flour.

Preheat the oven to 350°F. Lightly grease an 8-inch square pan with cooking spray and line it with parchment paper, leaving about 2 inches of overhang on two sides.

In a food processor, pulse together the flour, margarine, granulated sugar, and salt until crumbly. Set aside 1 cup of the dough and press the remainder into the prepared pan. Bake for about 18 minutes, until set. Let cool.

Carefully spread the jam over the baked crust. Crumble the reserved dough over the top, leaving some in larger clumps so some of the jam is peeking through. Bake for about 30 minutes, until the shortbread crumble is golden. Let cool, then refrigerate for at least 3 hours or up to overnight to firm up.

When the bars are chilled and set, lift them from the pan using the overhanging parchment paper as handles and set them on a cutting board. Using a sharp knife, cut into 2-inch squares, dust with confectioners' sugar, and serve.

BLACK FOREST CHERRY CAKE

SCHWARZWALDER KIRSCHTORTE

MAKES ONE 9-INCH CAKE

chocolate cake

3 cups all-purpose **flour**

2 cups **granulated sugar**

⅔ cup **unsweetened cocoa powder**

2 teaspoons **baking soda**

1 teaspoon **sea salt**

2 cups canned **coconut milk**, mixed well (see Tip, page 15)

1 cup **vegetable oil**

¼ cup **apple cider vinegar**

1 tablespoon **pure vanilla extract**

cherry filling

16 ounces **frozen cherries**

¼ cup **granulated sugar**

2 tablespoons **kirsch** or **brandy**

2 teaspoons **pure vanilla extract**

Ben's favorite cake is Black Forest Cherry Cake because his grandma, who was born in Germany, would always make it for him. I "surprise" him with it on his birthday every year. With a few of his birthdays under my belt, I've finally perfected the ultimate vegan version of this traditional cake.

MAKE-AHEAD TIP: The cake layers can be made in advance and frozen, unfrosted, for up to 1 month. Thaw and frost before serving.

MAKE IT GLUTEN-FREE: Use gluten-free baking flour, gluten-free cocoa powder, and gluten-free chocolate chips.

Make the cake: Preheat the oven to 350°F. Lightly grease two 9-inch round cake pans with cooking spray and line the bottoms with parchment paper cut to fit.

In a large bowl, whisk together the flour, granulated sugar, cocoa powder, baking soda, and salt. In a medium bowl, whisk together the coconut milk, oil, vinegar, and vanilla. Add the wet ingredients to the dry and whisk until just combined. Do not overmix.

Divide the batter evenly between the prepared cake pans. Bake, rotating the pans halfway through, for about 30 minutes, or until toothpicks inserted into the center of the cakes come out clean with a few crumbs clinging to them. Remove from the oven and let cool completely in the pans.

Meanwhile, make the cherry filling: In a small saucepan, combine the cherries, granulated sugar, and kirsch. Bring to a boil over medium heat and cook, stirring frequently, for 5 to 10 minutes, until the mixture is thick and saucy. Transfer to a small bowl, stir in the vanilla, and let cool. Taste, and add another splash of liquor, if desired.

frosting

2 cups **nonhydrogenated vegetable shortening**

4 cups **confectioners' sugar**

1 teaspoon **pure vanilla extract**

Almond milk, as needed

chocolate ganache

1 cup **vegan chocolate chips**

¼ cup **coconut milk** or **almond milk** (see Tip, page 15)

2 tablespoons **vegetable** or **coconut oil**

Make the frosting: In a stand mixer fitted with the whisk or paddle attachment or in a large bowl using a handheld mixer, beat the shortening until smooth. With the mixer running on low, add the confectioners' sugar and vanilla and beat to incorporate. Beat on high for about 2 minutes more, until light and fluffy. If needed, add a little almond milk, 1 tablespoon at a time, to thin the frosting.

Make the chocolate ganache: In the top of a double boiler, melt the chocolate chips and coconut milk. (Alternatively, put the chocolate chips and coconut milk in a small microwave-safe bowl and microwave in 15-second intervals, stirring after each, until melted and smooth.) Whisk in the vegetable oil until smooth.

When the cakes have cooled completely, run a knife around the inside edge of each pan to loosen the cakes and gently unmold them. Peel off the parchment paper. Place one cake on a serving plate, bottom-side up. Spoon on half of the cherry filling, drizzling the liquid evenly over it. Dollop the frosting on top of the cherry filling. Carefully spread the frosting, but don't worry if it's not perfect—the weight of the second cake layer will even it out. Place the second cake layer on top of the first, bottom-side up, and spread the chocolate ganache evenly over the top. Top with the remaining cherry filling.

CHOCOLATE CHIP PUMPKIN BREAD

MAKES 1 LOAF

2 cups all-purpose **flour**, plus more for dusting

1 cup **granulated sugar**

1 teaspoon **baking powder**

½ teaspoon **baking soda**

1 teaspoon **sea salt**

1 tablespoon **pumpkin pie spice**

1 cup canned **pure pumpkin puree**

1 cup canned **coconut milk**, mixed well (see Tip, page 15)

½ cup **vegetable oil**

2 teaspoons **apple cider vinegar**

1 tablespoon **pure vanilla extract**

1 cup **vegan chocolate chips**

Confectioners' sugar, for dusting

This recipe is super simple and fills your home with the scent of pumpkin spice, so it's my go-to for dinner parties and potlucks during the holidays. It's perfect when you want something a little more festive than banana bread that can be eaten at breakfast, lunch, or dinner.

MAKE-AHEAD TIP: The loaf can be made in advance and frozen for up to 1 month. Thaw and dust with confectioners' sugar before serving.

NOTE: For a quicker baking time, make these into cupcakes or mini cupcakes. The baking time will be 8 to 10 minutes for mini cupcakes and about 18 minutes for standard cupcakes.

MAKE IT GLUTEN-FREE: Use gluten-free baking flour and gluten-free chocolate chips.

Preheat the oven to 350°F. Lightly grease a 10 x 5-inch loaf pan with cooking spray and lightly dust with flour.

In a large bowl, whisk together the flour, granulated sugar, baking powder, baking soda, salt, and pumpkin pie spice. In a medium bowl, whisk together the pumpkin puree, coconut milk, oil, vinegar, and vanilla. Add the wet ingredients to the dry and whisk until just combined. Do not overmix. Gently fold in the chocolate chips.

Fill the prepared pan with the batter and smooth the top. Bake, rotating the pan halfway through, for 1 hour, or until a toothpick inserted into the center of the cake comes out clean with a few crumbs clinging to it. Let cool completely before unmolding.

Slice and dust with confectioners' sugar.

ESPRESSO CHOCOLATE CAKE

MAKES 1 BUNDT CAKE

cake

2¼ cups all-purpose **flour**

1½ cups **granulated sugar**

½ cup **unsweetened cocoa powder**

1½ teaspoons **baking soda**

¾ teaspoon **sea salt**

1½ cups canned **coconut milk**, mixed well (see Tip, page 15)

¾ cup **vegetable oil**

3 tablespoons **apple cider vinegar**

1 tablespoon **pure vanilla extract**

1 tablespoon **instant espresso powder**

glaze

3 tablespoons **water**

1 tablespoon **instant espresso powder**

2 cups **confectioners' sugar**

2 tablespoons **vegan margarine** or unrefined **coconut oil**, melted

2 teaspoons **pure vanilla extract**

On my twenty-ninth birthday, I decided to invite a few girlfriends over for dinner. I cooked a feast and also made myself this birthday cake. Some people think it's weird to make your own birthday cake, but I think it's fabulous. No one knows what you like better than *you!* So make this cake for yourself or for someone special.

MAKE-AHEAD TIP: The cake can be made in advance and frozen, unglazed, for up to 1 month. Thaw and glaze before serving.

MAKE IT GLUTEN-FREE: Use gluten-free baking flour and gluten-free cocoa powder.

Make the cake: Preheat the oven to 350°F. Generously grease a large Bundt pan with cooking spray.

In a large bowl, whisk together the flour, granulated sugar, cocoa powder, baking soda, and salt. In a medium bowl, whisk together the coconut milk, oil, vinegar, vanilla, and espresso powder. Add the wet ingredients to the dry and whisk until just combined. Do not overmix.

Fill the prepared pan evenly with the batter. Bake, rotating the pan halfway through, for about 45 minutes, or until a toothpick inserted into the center of the cake comes out clean with a few crumbs clinging to it.

Make the glaze: Just before assembling the cake, in a medium bowl, stir together the water and espresso powder and mix until dissolved. Add the confectioners' sugar, melted margarine, and vanilla. Whisk until smooth.

When the cake has cooled completely, run a knife around the inside edges.of the pan to loosen. Gently unmold the cake onto a serving plate and pour the glaze over the top.

OATMEAL CAKE WITH COCONUT CARAMEL GLAZE

MAKES ONE 8-INCH CAKE

cake

1½ cups all-purpose **flour**

¾ cup **granulated sugar**

½ teaspoon **baking soda**

½ teaspoon **baking powder**

½ teaspoon **sea salt**

¾ cup canned **coconut milk**, mixed well (see Tip, page 15)

½ cup **vegetable oil**

2 tablespoons **apple cider vinegar**

2 teaspoons **pure vanilla extract**

½ cup **rolled oats**

½ cup **shredded coconut**

glaze

½ cup **vegan margarine**

1 cup packed **light brown sugar**

¼ cup canned **coconut milk**, mixed well (see Tip, page 15), plus more as needed

1 teaspoon **pure vanilla extract**

Shredded coconut, for garnish

I invited some of my college friends over for dinner and made this cake along with a few other desserts (I never make just one dessert for a dinner party). Guess what? This was the hands-down standout favorite, even up against a decadent chocolate cake! The girls couldn't stop raving about it and fought over who got to take the last piece home to their boyfriend. My friend Nancy said it best: "Holy moly, the modest little oatmeal cake that steals the show!"

MAKE-AHEAD TIP: The cake can be made in advance and frozen, unglazed, for up to 1 month. Thaw and glaze before serving.

MAKE IT GLUTEN-FREE: Use gluten-free baking flour and gluten-free oats.

Make the cake: Preheat the oven to 350°F. Lightly grease an 8-inch square cake pan with cooking spray and line the bottom with parchment paper cut to fit.

In a large bowl, whisk together the flour, granulated sugar, baking soda, baking powder, and salt. In a medium bowl, whisk together the coconut milk, oil, vinegar, and vanilla. Add the wet ingredients to the dry and whisk until just combined. Do not overmix. Fold in the oats and coconut.

Fill the prepared cake pan with the batter and smooth the top. Bake, rotating the pan halfway through, for 30 to 35 minutes, or until a toothpick inserted into the center of the cake comes out clean with a few crumbs clinging to it. Remove from the oven and let cool completely.

Meanwhile, make the glaze: In a stand mixer fitted with the whisk attachment or in a large bowl using a handheld mixer, beat together the margarine and brown sugar for about 2 minutes, until fluffy. Add the coconut milk and vanilla and beat again. Add more coconut milk, 1 tablespoon at a time, as needed, and continue to beat until glaze is smooth and spreadable.

When the cake has cooled completely, gently unmold it onto a serving plate. Spread a layer of the glaze on top. Garnish with more shredded coconut and serve.

MARBLE POUND CAKE

MAKES 1 LOAF

2 cups all-purpose **flour**, plus more for dusting

½ cup **granulated sugar**

¼ cup packed **light brown sugar**

1 teaspoon **baking soda**

1 teaspoon **baking powder**

½ teaspoon **sea salt**

1 cup plus 3 tablespoons canned **coconut milk**, mixed well (see Tip, page 15)

½ cup **vegetable oil**

1 tablespoon **apple cider vinegar**

1 tablespoon **pure vanilla extract**

1 cup **vegan chocolate chips**

2 tablespoons **unsweetened cocoa powder**

As a girl who loves both chocolate and vanilla, I'm always enticed by the mesmerizing swirl of marble pound cake displayed at the registers of bakeries and coffee shops. Unfortunately, it's never vegan. So I took matters into my own hands. The result? Delicious homemade pound cake that's surely fresher and fluffier than the ones sitting in any bakery case!

MAKE-AHEAD TIP: The loaf can be made in advance and frozen for up to 1 month.

MAKE IT GLUTEN-FREE: Use gluten-free baking flour, gluten-free chocolate chips, and gluten-free cocoa powder.

Preheat the oven to 350°F. Lightly grease a 10 x 5-inch loaf pan with cooking spray and lightly dust with flour.

In a large bowl, whisk together the flour, granulated sugar, brown sugar, baking soda, baking powder, and salt. In a medium bowl, whisk together 1 cup of the coconut milk, oil, vinegar, and vanilla. Add the wet ingredients to the dry and whisk until just combined. Do not overmix. Gently fold in the chocolate chips.

Transfer ½ cup of the batter to a small bowl and whisk in the cocoa powder and remaining 3 tablespoons of coconut milk until incorporated.

Fill the prepared pan with the vanilla batter and top with the chocolate batter. Using a knife or chopstick, gently swirl the chocolate batter into the vanilla batter. Bake for about 1 hour, or until a toothpick inserted into the center of the cake comes out clean with a few crumbs clinging to it. Let the cake cool, then invert onto a serving plate, slice, and serve.

CHOCOLATE STRAWBERRY SHORTCAKE CUPCAKES

MAKES 14 CUPCAKES

cupcakes

1½ cups all-purpose **flour**

1 cup **granulated sugar**

⅓ cup **unsweetened cocoa powder**

1 teaspoon **baking soda**

½ teaspoon **sea salt**

1 cup canned **coconut milk**, mixed well (see Tip, page 15)

½ cup **vegetable oil**

2 tablespoons **apple cider vinegar**

2 teaspoons **pure vanilla extract**

frosting

2 cups **nonhydrogenated vegetable shortening**

4 cups **confectioners' sugar**

1 teaspoon **pure vanilla extract**

Almond milk, as needed

1½ cups hulled, sliced **fresh strawberries**, for garnish

Confectioners' sugar, for garnish

These cupcakes won first prize on Food Network's *Cupcake Wars*, which was pretty much the start of my culinary career. These cupcakes are unique and different-looking, award-winning in flavor, and basically symbolize all of my vegan hopes and dreams in a cupcake wrapper. I hope they are as special and lucky for you as they are for me.

MAKE-AHEAD TIP: The cupcakes can be made in advance and frozen, unfrosted, for up to 1 month. Thaw and frost before serving.

MAKE IT GLUTEN-FREE: Use gluten-free baking flour and gluten-free cocoa powder.

Make the cupcakes: Preheat the oven to 350°F. Line two 12-cup muffin pans with 14 cupcake liners.

In a large bowl, whisk together the flour, granulated sugar, cocoa powder, baking soda, and salt. In a medium bowl, whisk together the coconut milk, oil, vinegar, and vanilla. Add the wet ingredients to the dry and whisk until just combined. Do not overmix.

Fill the cupcake liners about two-thirds of the way full with the batter. Bake for 18 to 20 minutes, or until a toothpick inserted into the center of a cupcake comes out clean with a few crumbs clinging to it.

Make the frosting: In a stand mixer fitted with the whisk attachment, beat the shortening until smooth. With the mixer running on low, add the confectioners' sugar and vanilla and beat to incorporate. Beat on high for about 2 minutes more, until light and fluffy. If needed, add a little almond milk to thin the frosting.

When the cupcakes have cooled completely, slice off the top of each cupcake, reserving them. Pipe or spread a layer of frosting on top of the cut side of the cupcake, decorate with the sliced strawberries, and replace the top of the cupcake. Dust with confectioners' sugar, then top each cupcake with a dollop of frosting and a few more slices of strawberry.

BANANA DOUGHNUTS
WITH MAPLE GLAZE
MAKES 8 DOUGHNUTS

doughnuts

1⅓ cups all-purpose **flour**

⅓ cup **granulated sugar**

1 teaspoon **baking soda**

1 teaspoon **ground nutmeg**

½ teaspoon **sea salt**

½ cup **almond milk**

½ cup mashed **banana** (about 1 banana)

2 tablespoons **vegetable oil**

2 tablespoons **apple cider vinegar**

1 teaspoon **pure vanilla extract**

glaze

1 cup **confectioners' sugar**

1 tablespoon **almond milk**, plus more as needed

1 tablespoon **pure maple syrup**

1 teaspoon **pure maple extract**

These banana doughnuts are baked, not fried, making them perfect for a healthier breakfast or light dessert. Banana and maple is a classic combo. To jazz these up, you can add chocolate chips into the doughnuts or decorate the tops with sprinkles, or you could stay a maple purist like me!

MAKE IT GLUTEN-FREE: Use gluten-free baking flour.

Make the doughnuts: Preheat the oven to 375°F. Lightly grease a doughnut pan with cooking spray.

In a large bowl, whisk together the flour, granulated sugar, baking soda, nutmeg, and salt. In a medium bowl, whisk together the almond milk, banana, oil, vinegar, and vanilla. Add the wet ingredients to the dry and whisk together until just combined. Do not overmix.

Transfer the batter to a pastry bag or a zip-top plastic bag, then cut off one corner. Pipe the batter into the prepared doughnut pans and bake for 10 to 12 minutes, until the tops look set. Remove the pan from the oven and let the doughnuts sit for at least 5 minutes before unmolding.

Make the glaze: In a small bowl, whisk together all the glaze ingredients until smooth. If the glaze seems too thick, add more almond milk, 1 teaspoon at a time, to thin it.

To assemble, dip the top of each doughnut into the glaze. Twist the doughnut as you remove it from the glaze to give it a nice finish and prevent drips.

CHOCOLATE BOURBON WALNUT PIE

MAKES ONE 9-INCH PIE

¾ cup all-purpose **flour**

¾ cup **sugar**

1 teaspoon **baking powder**

½ cup **vegan margarine**, melted

¼ cup **bourbon**

1 teaspoon **pure vanilla extract**

1 cup chopped **walnuts**

1¼ cups **vegan chocolate chips**

1 (9-inch) **vegan piecrust**, store-bought frozen or homemade (recipe follows)

This is essentially gooey, chocolaty pecan pie with an earthy hint of bourbon—commonly known as Derby Pie—but my version features walnuts. The brown sugary filling is sweet, nutty, and reminiscent of cookie dough. The filling is super simple and comes together in one bowl, so it's the perfect quick dessert for a dinner party.

Preheat the oven to 350°F.

In a large bowl, whisk together the flour, sugar, and baking powder. In a small bowl, whisk together the melted margarine, bourbon, and vanilla. Add the wet ingredients to the dry and whisk until just combined. Fold in the walnuts and chocolate chips.

Spread the filling into the piecrust and bake for about 55 minutes, until set. Let cool slightly before serving.

vegan piecrust

MAKES ONE 9-INCH PIECRUST

1¼ cups all-purpose **flour**, plus more for dusting

1½ teaspoons **sugar**

½ teaspoon **sea salt**

½ cup **nonhydrogenated vegetable shortening** or **vegan margarine**

5 tablespoons **ice water**, as needed

You can make the dough by hand or using a food processor.

By hand: In a medium bowl, whisk together the flour, sugar, and salt. Using a pastry cutter, cut the shortening into the flour until the mixture has a crumbly consistency. Add the ice water, 1 tablespoon at a time, and mix with a spoon until the dough just holds together. You may not need to use all the water. Do not overwork the dough.

Using a food processor: Put the flour, sugar, and salt in the food processor. Pulse until the ingredients are combined. Add the shortening and pulse until the mixture has a crumbly consistency. Add the ice water, 1 tablespoon at a time, and pulse until the dough just holds together. You may not need to use all the water. Do not overprocess the dough.

Form the dough into a disc and cover in plastic wrap. Store in the refrigerator until ready to use, up to 3 days. If the dough is difficult to roll, let it soften at room temperature until it is easier to work with. Once you are ready to roll, lightly dust your work surface with flour and use a rolling pin to roll the dough into a large circle, about ¼ inch thick. Once rolled out, the dough can be wrapped in plastic and stored in the freezer for up to 1 month.

BLACKBERRY COBBLER WITH VANILLA ICE CREAM

SERVES 8

dough

1⅓ cups all-purpose **flour**

2 tablespoons **sugar**, plus more for sprinkling

1½ teaspoons **baking powder**

½ teaspoon **sea salt**

¼ cup **vegan margarine** or **coconut oil**, melted

½ cup **almond milk**, plus more for brushing

berries

½ cup **sugar**

2 tablespoons all-purpose **flour**

1 teaspoon **ground cinnamon**

16 to 20 ounces **frozen blackberries**

Vanilla Ice Cream (recipe follows), for serving

When I'm having friends over for dinner and I want to make an easy dessert that doesn't require a ton of bowls or equipment, I always turn to this cobbler. It's so easy to grab a bag of frozen berries from the grocery store and whip up this cobbler topping. For a shortcut, you can top it with store-bought vegan ice cream.

MAKE IT GLUTEN-FREE: Use gluten-free baking flour.

Preheat the oven to 375°F. Lightly grease an 8-inch square baking pan or six ramekins with cooking spray.

Make the dough: In a medium bowl, whisk together the flour, sugar, baking powder, and salt. In a small bowl, whisk together the melted margarine and almond milk. Add the wet ingredients to the dry and mix with a wooden spoon until combined. The dough will be sticky. Do not overmix.

Make the berries: In a medium bowl, whisk together the sugar, flour, and cinnamon. Add the blackberries and toss with a large spoon to coat. Transfer the blackberries to the prepared pan.

Using a tablespoon, scoop lumps of the dough on top of the blackberries, leaving the berries peeking through. Brush the top of the dough with almond milk and generously sprinkle with sugar.

Bake, rotating the pan halfway through, for about 1 hour, or until the dough is thoroughly cooked and lightly browned on top. Let the cobbler sit for at least 5 to 10 minutes before serving with ice cream.

vanilla ice cream

MAKES ABOUT 1 PINT

¼ cup **raw cashews** (see Tip, page 11)

1 (13.5-ounce) can **coconut milk**

½ cup **agave nectar**

1 tablespoon refined **coconut oil**

2 teaspoons **pure vanilla extract**

Pinch of **sea salt**

¼ teaspoon **xanthan gum**

In a blender, combine the cashews, coconut milk, agave, coconut oil, vanilla, and salt and blend on high speed for about 2 minutes, until completely smooth. Add the xanthan gum and blend again on high speed to incorporate. Cover and refrigerate until cold. Transfer the mixture to an ice cream maker and churn according to the manufacturer's instructions. Transfer to an airtight container and press plastic wrap directly against the surface of the ice cream before affixing the lid. Store in the freezer for as long as it lasts!

BIRTHDAY CAKE

MAKES ONE 9-INCH CAKE

cake

3 cups all-purpose **flour**

1½ cups **granulated sugar**

1 teaspoon **baking soda**

1 teaspoon **baking powder**

1 teaspoon **sea salt**

1½ cups canned **coconut milk**, mixed well (see Tip, page 15)

1 cup **vegetable oil**

¼ cup **apple cider vinegar**

1 tablespoon **pure vanilla extract**

frosting

2 cups **nonhydrogenated vegetable shortening**

4 cups **confectioners' sugar**

2 teaspoons **pure vanilla extract**

Almond milk, as needed

Natural food dye (optional)

Rainbow sprinkles (I like Sweetapolita, see page 17) or edible flowers, for garnish (optional)

This is my go-to vanilla cake for birthdays (or regular days). Have fun with coloring or flavoring the frosting, and decorate it to your vegan heart's content! Edible flowers are a great way to dress up this cake or even make it suitable to be a wedding cake.

MAKE IT GLUTEN-FREE: Use gluten-free baking flour.

Make the cake: Preheat the oven to 350°F. Lightly grease two 9-inch round cake pans with cooking spray and line the bottoms with parchment paper cut to fit.

In a large bowl, whisk together the flour, granulated sugar, baking soda, baking powder, and salt. In a medium bowl, whisk together the coconut milk, oil, vinegar, and vanilla. Add the wet ingredients to the dry and whisk until just combined. Do not overmix.

Divide the batter evenly between the prepared pans. Bake, rotating the pans halfway through, for 28 to 30 minutes, or until toothpicks inserted into the centers of the cakes come out clean with a few crumbs clinging to them. Let the cakes cool completely in the pans.

Meanwhile, make the frosting: In a stand mixer fitted with the whisk or paddle attachment or in a large bowl using a handheld mixer, beat the shortening until smooth. With the mixer running on low, add the confectioners' sugar and vanilla and beat to incorporate. Beat on high speed for about 2 minutes more, until light and fluffy. If needed, add a little almond milk to thin the frosting. If desired, add food dye to color.

When the cakes have cooled completely, run a knife around the inside edge of each pan to loosen and gently unmold the cakes. Peel off the parchment paper. Place one cake on a serving plate, bottom-side up. Spread a layer of frosting over the cake. Place the second cake on top of the first, also bottom-side up, and spread another layer of frosting on top. Fully or partially frost the sides, top with sprinkles or edible flowers, as desired.

CHOCOLATE SUPERFOOD ICE CREAM

SERVES 8

1 (13.5-ounce) can **coconut milk**

½ cup **agave nectar**

¼ cup **raw cashews** (see Tip, page 11)

¼ cup **gluten-free unsweetened cocoa powder**

1 tablespoon refined **coconut oil**

1 teaspoon **pure vanilla extract**

Pinch of **sea salt**

¼ cup **goji berries**

¼ cup **shredded coconut**

¼ cup **cacao nibs**

2 tablespoons **chia seeds**

This is my favorite ice cream flavor in the whole vegan world. Goji berries, cacao nibs, raw coconut, and chia seeds are all superfoods with incredible nutritional properties, which makes this ice cream a complete and total upgrade from any ordinary chocolate with sprinkles or gummy bears. Don't tell, but sometimes I eat it for breakfast—is that really any different than eating chia pudding?

In a blender, combine the coconut milk, agave, cashews, cocoa powder, coconut oil, vanilla, and salt and blend on high speed for about 2 minutes, until completely smooth. Refrigerate until cold.

Transfer the mixture to an ice cream maker and churn according to the manufacturer's instructions. Fold in the goji berries, shredded coconut, cacao nibs, and chia using a spatula. Transfer to an airtight container and press plastic wrap directly against the surface of the ice cream before affixing the lid. Store in the freezer for as long as it lasts!

GEORGIA PEACH PIE

MAKES ONE 9-INCH PIE

½ cup **sugar**, plus more for sprinkling

2 tablespoons all-purpose **flour**

1 teaspoon **ground cinnamon**

16 to 20 ounces **frozen peach slices**, or 5 **fresh peaches**, pitted and sliced

2 (9-inch) **vegan piecrusts**, store-bought frozen or homemade (page 243), at room temperature

Almond milk, for brushing

Vanilla ice cream, store-bought or homemade (page 245)

When I'm in the mood for a fruit dessert, this peach pie is always my answer. It is so simple and doesn't leave a lot of dirty dishes. Sweet, tangy, juicy peaches are irresistible during the summer, but frozen peaches allow you to enjoy this pie all year round.

Preheat the oven to 375°F. Lightly grease a 9-inch pie pan with cooking spray, and place one of the piecrusts inside.

In a large bowl, whisk together the sugar, flour, and cinnamon. Add the peaches and mix with a large spoon to coat. Pour the filling into the piecrust in the pan.

Remove the second piecrust from its packaging. Lay it over the peaches and gently press down. The crust will likely crack and look very imperfect—that's okay. Crimp the dough edges between your index fingers to make a decorative border, using almond milk to smooth the edges of the two crusts together. Cut four slits in the top crust.

Brush the top and edges of the piecrust with almond milk and sprinkle generously with sugar for an extra-sweet and crisp top. Bake for 50 to 55 minutes, until the crust is nicely browned. Serve warm, with ice cream.

LEMON CHEESECAKE WITH WILD BLUEBERRY SAUCE

MAKES ONE 9-INCH CHEESECAKE

crust

1 cup **pecans**

1 cup pitted **Medjool dates**

2 teaspoons **pure vanilla extract**

Pinch of **sea salt**

filling

1 (13.5-ounce) can **coconut milk**

1 cup **raw cashews** (see Tip, page 11)

½ cup **agave nectar** or **pure maple syrup**

¼ cup refined **coconut oil**

2 teaspoons **pure vanilla extract**

¼ teaspoon **sea salt**

Zest and juice of 1 **lemon**

Wild Blueberry Sauce (recipe follows)

This is one of my most impressive desserts. My mom and I developed the recipe together, and my dad and brother go crazy over it. The ingredients are simple, fresh, and mostly raw, so the flavors are very bright. And the colors are gorgeous once the wild blueberry sauce hits the cheesecake. Say good-bye to diner cheesecake and hello to this luscious, silky homemade version!

NOTE: The cheesecake will be best if chilled in the freezer for at least 8 hours or overnight before serving.

Lightly grease a 9-inch springform pan or round cake pan with cooking spray. If you're using a cake pan, line the bottom with parchment paper cut to fit.

Make the crust: In a food processor, combine all the crust ingredients and process until the pecans and dates are finely chopped and the mixture is combined. Transfer the mixture to the prepared pan and press it into the pan firmly and evenly.

Make the filling: Combine the coconut milk, cashews, agave, coconut oil, vanilla, salt, and lemon juice in a blender and blend on high speed for about 2 minutes, until very smooth. Stir in the lemon zest. Pour the filling on top of the crust and chill in the freezer for at least 8 hours or up to overnight, until completely firm.

To serve, remove the cheesecake from the freezer and release the sides of the springform pan or gently run a knife around the edges of the cake pan. Unmold or cut slices directly from the pan using a sharp knife. Top each slice with Wild Blueberry Sauce and serve. Return any leftover cheesecake to the freezer immediately so it does not melt.

wild blueberry sauce

MAKES 1 CUP

1 (10-ounce) bag **frozen wild blueberries**

2 tablespoons **water**

¼ cup **sugar**

1 teaspoon **lemon juice**

Pinch of **sea salt**

In a medium saucepan, combine the blueberries, water, sugar, lemon juice, and salt. Cook, stirring frequently, over medium heat for about 15 minutes, or until thick and saucy. Store in an airtight container in the refrigerator for up to 5 days.

PISTACHIO ICE CREAM

SERVES 4

½ cup **water**

½ cup **raw shelled pistachios**

1 cup canned **coconut milk**, mixed well (see Tip, page 15)

½ cup **agave nectar**

1 tablespoon refined **coconut oil**

2 teaspoons **pure almond extract**

Pinch of **sea salt**

¼ teaspoon **xanthan gum**

¼ cup shelled chopped **pistachios** (see Tip)

hot fudge

½ cup canned **coconut milk**, mixed well (see Tip, page 15)

1 cup **vegan gluten-free chocolate chips**

1 tablespoon **agave nectar**

½ teaspoon **pure vanilla extract**

I used to *love* pistachio ice cream as a kid. And I thought it was healthy because it was made with nuts. Well, not quite. But this version *is* much healthier than the traditional because the ingredients are all natural, and the color and creaminess actually comes from raw pistachios instead of dairy, green food dye, and artificial sweeteners. Serve this ice cream scooped into a cup or cone, or follow the directions to make it into a hot fudge sundae.

In a blender, combine the water, shelled pistachios, coconut milk, agave, coconut oil, almond extract, and salt and blend on high speed for about 2 minutes, until completely smooth. Add the xanthan gum and blend again on high speed to incorporate. Refrigerate until cold.

Transfer the mixture to an ice cream maker and churn according to the manufacturer's instructions. Fold the chopped pistachios into the ice cream. Transfer to an airtight container and press plastic wrap directly against the surface of the ice cream before affixing the lid. Freeze until ready to serve.

Make the hot fudge: Just before serving, in a small saucepan, heat the coconut milk over medium-high heat until it just boils. Reduce the heat to low and whisk in the chocolate chips. Cook, whisking frequently, 2 to 3 minutes, until smooth. Remove the pot from the heat and whisk in the agave and vanilla.

Scoop the ice cream into bowls, top with hot fudge, and serve.

TIP SIFTING NUTS

After I chop nuts (either by hand or by pulsing in a food processor), I like to transfer them to a mesh strainer to sift out any small, dustlike particles so only substantial chopped nuts remain, providing a nice crunch.

VANILLA GLAZED
DOUGHNUT HOLES
MAKES ABOUT 24 DOUGHNUT HOLES

doughnuts

2⅔ cups all-purpose **flour**

⅔ cup **granulated sugar**

2 teaspoons **baking soda**

¼ teaspoon **ground nutmeg**

1 teaspoon **sea salt**

1 cup **almond milk**

¼ cup **vegetable oil**, plus more for frying

¼ cup **apple cider vinegar**

2 teaspoons **pure vanilla extract**

glaze

2 cups **confectioners' sugar**

5 tablespoons **almond milk**

1 teaspoon **pure vanilla extract**

Vegan rainbow sprinkles (I like Sweetapolita, see page 17), for garnish

My friend Esha was going through a "doughnut phase" one year, so for her birthday, my roommate Daniella and I made these for her. We brought them to her birthday party at an Italian restaurant, and all the guests were looking over at our table because they wanted to order the doughnuts! These doughnuts are cute enough for any celebration, and the aforementioned Italian restaurant should probably put them on their menu.

NOTE: The dough is best if chilled for at least 3 hours or up to overnight.

Make the doughnuts: In a large bowl, whisk together the flour, granulated sugar, baking soda, nutmeg, and salt. In a medium bowl, whisk together the almond milk, oil, vinegar, and vanilla. Add the wet ingredients to the dry and stir together until just combined. Do not overmix. Refrigerate the batter, covered, for at least 3 hours or up to overnight.

Fill a large, deep-sided skillet or deep fryer with about 2 inches of oil. Heat the oil to 350°F, or until a small spoonful of batter sizzles when added. Using a cookie scoop, scoop about 1½ tablespoons of the batter and carefully drop it into the hot oil. Do not overcrowd the pan; work in batches and allow the oil to return to 350°F between batches. Fry for about 3 minutes, turning the doughnut holes as soon as they hit the oil and occasionally thereafter, until crispy and lightly browned all over. Test for doneness by cutting into a doughnut to make sure it is cooked through. If the doughnuts begin to lose their shape when frying, refrigerate the batter for about 10 minutes before frying the next batch. Remove from the oil with a slotted spoon or spider and drain on paper towels.

Make the glaze: In a small bowl, whisk together the confectioners' sugar, almond milk, and vanilla until smooth. If the sugar does not completely dissolve, let the mixture sit for a few minutes, then whisk again. Put the sprinkles in a small bowl.

Roll the doughnuts through the glaze, then roll them in sprinkles to coat. Serve warm.

BONE APPÉTIT!

MAKES ABOUT 24 (3-INCH) BONES

2 cups **whole-wheat flour**, plus more for dusting

1 cup cooked mashed **sweet potato** (about 1 medium sweet potato)

¼ cup **water**, plus more as needed

These treats are for the pups! My rescue Chi babies, Winnie and Buster, give these bones two paws up, likely because they love sweet potato just like their mommy. This also makes a cute gift for any friend with a fur baby.

Preheat the oven to 300°F. Line a large baking sheet with parchment paper.

In a large bowl, combine the flour, sweet potato, and water and mix using your hands until well combined. Add more water, 1 tablespoon at a time, if needed to bring the dough together.

Turn out the mixture onto a lightly floured surface and roll or pat into a ¼-inch-thick rectangle. Cut the treats out using a 3-inch bone-shaped cookie cutter (or any shape cutter) and place on the prepared baking sheet. Reroll the scraps and repeat to make as many bones as possible.

Bake for about 40 minutes, then turn off the heat and let the bones sit in the closed oven for another hour to help them crisp up. Let cool to room temperature before serving them to your pet. Store in an airtight container in a cool, dry place for up to 5 days.

ACKNOWLEDGMENTS

A million thanks and vegan cupcakes to . . .

My visionary editor, Amanda Englander, for pouring your heart into every page of this book. I admire your unmatched attention to detail.

The entire Clarkson Potter family: Carisa Hays, Carly Gorga, Erica Gelbard, Jana Branson, Matthew Martin, Stephanie Huntwork, Terry Deal, Kim Tyner, and Sara Rennert.

The best literary agent in the entire world, Alyssa Reuben, and to Katelyn Dougherty and the rest of the Paradigm team.

My brilliant powerhouse publicist (and so much more), Brianne Perea.

Mommy, for testing all the recipes in this book by my side and believing in me even through moments when I stop believing in myself.

Daddy, for supporting my entrepreneurial dreams in every way possible, and for having the biggest heart and joining me in a lifestyle and diet to end animal suffering.

Ben, my #1 taste tester and Prince Charming, thank you for making me better, smarter, and stronger. Together we dream bigger than I ever could alone.

Andy and Rocio—everyone says my family must be so "lucky" to get to "taste test" my "amazing" creations. As you know, it's no easy task. Meal after meal, one failed attempt after another, too much salt, too little salt, too crunchy, too soft, here try this version, just one more bite . . . You guys take it like champs with unwavering support.

The girls I used to call my interns. Who became my chefs. Then my friends. Then my sisters. Now my genius culinary think tank/guardian angels who have carried me through my career on the toughest of days and never let me give up on the vegan dream. On days when the road turns scary and dark, there is nothing like having a brilliant group of women to light your way. Ann Marie Monteiro, Daniella De Santo, Elaina Kaufman, Star Calaman, Susan Antoniewicz, and Valerie DiClerico, I am so blessed to know you.

Extra thanks to my recipe-testing culinary rock stars Susan Antoniewicz and Ann Marie Monteiro, for bringing cheer and optimism to the most challenging days and always reminding me that cooking is fun. Thank you for pushing me to be the best version of myself and for never letting me settle for anything less. The recipes in this book are perfect because of you.

My detail-oriented super-chef, Nancy Wolfe, for testing the recipes in this book over and over and over again with unwavering enthusiasm. And to your taste testing MVP's: Jerry Feldman, Nancy and Bob Schwab; Linda, Jack, and Christy Massopust; and Beth and Derek Sampson.

Rishi Bhandari, Leah Vickers, and Rob Glunt, thank you for your friendship and for inspiring me to be fearless.

Sonia, Tina, Mahshid, and Hushmand Sohaili, thank you for your extreme generosity and for treating me like family.

My talented web designer, Aaron Lea, for being a creative force.

My soul sister, Lindsay Jill Roth, for your constant cheerleading.

To Chris Kerr, for being the brightest light in the vegan universe.

My braid guru, Kayley Pak, for role modeling the beauty of putting heart and soul into your craft.

Lisa Bloom and Braden Pollock, for being the most powerful, fun, and generous vegan duo on the planet. Lisa, I look up to you in more ways than I could ever list.

These inspiring vegan superwomen: Colleen Holland, Leanne Mai-Ly Hilgart, Elizabeth Dee, Emily Brobeck, Kenda Norris, and Daniella Yacobovsky.

My incredible photographer, Christina Holmes, you are not only the very best at your craft but you are also quite possibly the sweetest person I've met in the business. In moments where I've felt like my sweetness is a weakness, you remind me that it is indeed always a strength.

Artistic food stylist Eugene Jho, for fulfilling my dreams of having the sauciest, juiciest, crispiest, gooiest, drippiest cookbook in the world.

The ever-fabulous prop stylist Kalen Kaminski, for making this book chic and gorgeous down to every last napkin.

Michael Symon, for writing the incredible foreword to this book and for supporting my every move.

Trisha Yearwood, for inviting me into your home to cook and laugh with you and for sharing the best vegan tomato soup recipe on the planet.

And to Ava Bassi, Carma Munoz-North, Chef Barbara Rich, Jeff Fiala, Grandpa and Anna Maria, Josh Saviano, Katie Lee, Leslie Meredith, Lisa Grossman Ben-Tal, Matt and Matthew Monteiro, Michael Parrish Dudell, Nick Crowell, Rabbi Zev Schwartz, Robin DeMarco, Sandra Hakim, the Ghai family, the Natural Gourmet Institute, and Vijay Brihmadesam.

INDEX

Copyright © 2018 by CKC Sales, LLC
Photographs copyright © 2018 by
Christina Holmes

All rights reserved.
Published in the United States by
Clarkson Potter/Publishers, an imprint
of the Crown Publishing Group, a
division of Penguin Random House
LLC, New York.
crownpublishing.com
clarksonpotter.com

CLARKSON POTTER is a trademark
and POTTER with colophon is a regis-
tered trademark of Penguin Random
House LLC.

Library of Congress Cataloging-in-
Publication Data
Names: Coscarelli, Chloe, author.
Title: Chloe flavor : saucy, crispy,
spicy, vegan / Chloe Coscarelli ;
   photographs by Christina Holmes ;
foreword by Michael Symon.
Description: First edition. | New York :
Clarkson Potter/Publishers, [2018] |
   Includes index.
Identifiers: LCCN 2017021732| ISBN
9780451499622 (hardcover) | ISBN
   9780451499639 (ebook)
Subjects: LCSH: Vegan cooking. |
LCGFT: Cookbooks.
Classification: LCC TX837 .C6639
2018 | DDC 641.5/636—dc23 LC
record available at https://lccn.loc.
gov/2017021732

ISBN 978-0-451-49962-2
Ebook ISBN 978-0-451-49963-9

Printed in China

Book and cover design by
Stephanie Huntwork
Cover photography by
Christina Holmes

10 9 8 7 6 5 4 3 2 1

First Edition